CULTURE SMART!

EGYPT

THE ESSENTIAL GUIDE TO CUSTOMS & CULTURE

ISABELLA MORRIS

KUPERARD

"The real voyage of discovery consists not in seeking new landscapes, but in having new eyes."

Adapted from Marcel Proust, *Remembrance of Things Past.*

ISBN 978 1 78702 345 1

British Library Cataloguing in Publication Data
A CIP catalogue entry for this book is available
from the British Library

First published in Great Britain
by Kuperard, an imprint of Bravo Ltd
59 Hutton Grove, London N12 8DS
Tel: +44 (0) 20 8446 2440
www.culturesmart.co.uk
Inquiries: publicity@kuperard.co.uk

Design Bobby Birchall
Printed in Turkey

ISABELLA MORRIS is an award-winning writer and English teacher from South Africa who now lives in Alexandria, where she works as an editor and ghostwriter. She has an M.A. from the University of Witswatersrand, and has worked as a travel and feature writer, contributing articles to *The Sunday Independent* and *The Citizen*.

Isabella has been caving in the lava tubes of the volcano of Piton de la Fournaise on Réunion Island, and has done white-water rafting in Malawi and hot-air ballooning in Egypt's Valley of the Kings. Today she spends her leisure time walking on the Alexandria Corniche, sketching the old buildings, or people-watching in the bustling Mansheya district. Her latest published book is the short-story collection *What We Dare Not Say*, which has been translated and published in Arabic. She is the author of *Culture Smart! South Africa*, *Black Like You*, *Capitalist Crusader*, and *Conquering the Poverty of the Mind*, and has contributed to several anthologies of short stories.

CONTENTS

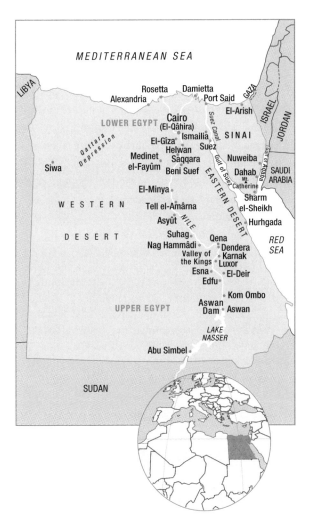

INTRODUCTION

To many, the idea of Egypt conjures up a picture of the great pyramids and Sphinx towering over the empty desert. But these monuments are merely the best known of many treasures left by the remarkable civilization of Ancient Egypt. For thousands of years the fertile banks of the Nile have been home to human settlement, and throughout its history Egypt has exchanged influences with the many different cultures it has encountered. Greeks, Romans, Persians, and Arabs have all left their mark on modern Egyptian society in the form of an astonishing legacy of temples, churches, and mosques.

At first sight, modern-day Egypt is an unruly and chaotic place, a cacophony of sounds, an overload of smells, and a visual theater, all of which can be taxing on the senses. Ancient church domes and medieval minarets share the same space with fast-food chains and internet cafés.

The country that has inspired conquerors, academics, and artists is home to 113 million people, who call it *Omm Eddunia*, Mother of the World. It is the people who are Egypt's true wealth. They are by nature friendly, cheerful, warm, and hospitable, renowned for their sense of humor, and extremely stubborn and proud. Good personal relations are at the core of the Egyptian value system. People are more important than time or money.

As in many developing countries, only certain aspects of this traditional and deeply conservative society have been affected by modernization. One can travel on excellent new highways, but villages still have dirt roads. Televisions in fashionable cafés play the latest football matches and music videos, while the call to prayer rings out from loudspeakers five times a day. In Egypt everyone finds their way of coping with change, while trying to uphold traditional values.

This new edition of *Culture Smart! Egypt* reveals a country coping with changes occasioned by both the post 2011 Revolution and the Covid-19 pandemic. The Revolution did not result in the sociopolitical reforms that the people had hoped for, and the pandemic impacted the country's socioeconomic landscape.

This book explores the codes and paradoxes of Egyptian life. It outlines the country's history and shows the forces that have shaped its sensibility. It explains people's values and attitudes and guides you through local customs and traditions. It opens a window into the private lives of Egyptians, how they behave at home, and how they interact with foreign visitors. It offers practical advice, from how to make friends to avoiding faux pas.

Culture Smart! Egypt sets out to make that first trip as rich as possible, to take you beyond the clichés to the real people. Welcome to Egypt, *Ahlan wa Sahlan*!

Official Name	Arab Republic of Egypt	Egypt is a member of the Arab League and the African Union.
Capital City	Cairo	Population approx. 7.7 million (excl. the Greater Cairo area)
Main Cities	Alexandria, Port Said, Suez, Asyût	
Population	113 million	Population growth rate 1.67%
Ethnic Makeup	Egyptian 95%. Minorities are the Berbers of the Siwa Oasis, Nubians along the southern Nile, Bedouins, and Copts who make up 5% of the total population.	
Age Structure	0–14 years: 33% 15–54 years: 62% 65 years and over: 5%	
Area	387,000 sq. miles (1,001,000 sq. km)	
Geography	Situated at northeast corner of Africa. Bordered by Libya, Sudan, Israel, and Gaza	Four regions: Delta and Nile Valley, Western Desert, Eastern Desert, Sinai Peninsula
Terrain	Desert plateau interrupted by Nile Valley and Delta	The Nile flows through the country, dividing at Cairo to form the Delta.
Climate	Hot, dry summers and mild winters	
Natural Resources	Petroleum, natural gas, iron ore, phosphates, manganese, limestone, gypsum, talc, asbestos, lead, zinc	

Currency	Egyptian pound (LE or EGP)	
Language	Arabic	English and French widely understood by educated classes
Religion	Mostly Sunni Muslim; approx.10% Christian, mainly Coptic	
Minority Faiths	Shi'a Muslim, Greek Orthodox and other Christians, Baha'i, Jewish	
Government	Egypt is a republic. Bicameral legislature. The president is the head of state, elected by popular vote for a six-year term.	
Media	Some television channels and newspapers are state owned. There are a number of privately owned satellite TV channels.	The three main government papers are *Al Ahram*, *Al Akhbar*, and *Al Gomhouria*. The liberal *Al-Masry Al-Youm* is independent.
Electricity	220 volts (50 Hz)	2-pronged plugs used
DVD/Video	TV/video is PAL system; DVD is European region	
Internet Domain	.eg	
Telephone	Egypt's country code is 20.	To dial out of Egypt, dial 00 and then the country code.
Time Zone	GMT +2 hours. During the summer it is GMT +3 hours.	

CHAPTER ONE

LAND & PEOPLE

GEOGRAPHY

Egypt's ancient monuments and artifacts have attracted travelers for millennia and today its modern society is a fusion of the old and new. The result is a multifaceted, multisensory experience for visitors. The Nile River was the central feature around which Ancient Egyptian civilization developed, and the river retains its essential role as most Egyptians still live in towns and cities along its banks. Many travelers often associate the terms Upper Egypt and Lower Egypt with the north and south of the country respectively. However, as the Nile flows from south to north, from a higher to a lower elevation, the south is Upper Egypt and the north Lower Egypt.

Situated on the northeastern tip of Africa, Egypt shares land borders with Libya to the west, Sudan to the south, and Israel and the Palestinian territory of Gaza on the east. With a coastline of 1,800 miles (2,900 km) that includes the Mediterranean Sea, the Gulf of Suez, and the Gulf of Aqaba, it has maritime borders to the north with Libya,

Cyprus, Greece, and Turkey, and with Jordan and Saudi Arabia to the east. The Suez Canal joins the Mediterranean and the natural eastern border of the Red Sea, which, unlike most of the country, falls within Asia.

The country lies generally at 50 feet (15.24 m) below sea level. Its highest point is Mount Catherine at 8,668 feet (2,642 m) above sea level, while its lowest point is the Qattara Depression at 436 feet (132.83m) below sea level.

Egypt is divided into four regions, three of which fall in the areas adjoining the Nile, namely the Nile Valley and Delta, the Western Desert, and the Eastern Desert. The arc or fan shape of the Nile River Valley resembles a lotus flower, the ancient Egyptian symbol for the regeneration of life. The long, narrow river valley is the stem, while the delta spreads out into the cup shape of the flower, and the area around Fayyum is the bud. The river empties into the Mediterranean Sea.

A traditional lateen-rigged *felucca* on the Nile at Aswan.

The fourth region, the Sinai Peninsula, lies east of the Suez Canal.

The Nile Delta, one of the world's largest river deltas, occupies an area of about 14,000 sq. miles (22,000 sq. km). It begins slightly downriver from Cairo, and runs 100 miles (160 km) to the east of Alexandria, fanning out across 150 miles (240 km) of Mediterranean coastline toward Port Said in the east. Agriculture flourished in the delta thanks to its rich nutrients; however, these days the land's productivity owes less to the flood plain's natural silt content than to chemical fertilizers and pesticides.

The Nile Valley is a 621 mile (1,000 km) long, narrow stretch of cultivated land that runs from Cairo to Aswan. This region is the greatest open-air museum in the world—a rich storehouse of ancient tombs and temples. The most prominent physical feature is the Aswan High Dam, one of the largest man-made dams in the world.

The Western Desert, the largest in Egypt at 259,000 square miles (671,000 sq. km), stretches from the Nile Valley into Libya, and is rich in mineral resources. Its relentless heat is broken by a series of green oases, the largest of which is Siwa, near the Libyan border.

The Eastern Desert is that part of the Sahara Desert east of the Nile River that stretches to the Red Sea and Gulf of Suez. It occupies almost a quarter of Egypt's land surface and is a barren plateau, indented occasionally by cliffs and mountains on its eastern edge. The area was historically a trade route, and used for the mining of semi-precious metals. Today it is predominantly mined for oil and gas.

The Sinai Peninsula is a large triangular wedge situated to the east of the Suez Canal. Its southern

Sunrise over Mount Sinai.

part is mountainous and includes Mount Catherine.
Heading north, the topography flattens out toward the
Mediterranean coast.

CLIMATE

Ninety-six percent of the Egyptian topography is a flat
desert plateau with vast, almost barren, areas interrupted
only by the fertile Nile Valley and Delta—a mere 4 percent
of the total area. As a result, Egypt's climate is generally hot
and dry. There is a brief spring in April, and summer lasts
from May to September, followed by a brief fall in October
and winter from November to March. Only the northern
cities on the eastern Mediterranean, such as Alexandria
and Rafah, enjoy some relief from the muggy summers
when the winter rains fall. Cooler night temperatures
are common in the Sinai mountainous region. While

prevailing northern winds moderate temperatures in the north, the desert interior offers little respite, and summer nights are typically hot.

Dry sandy seasonal winds, known as the *Khamsin* (Arabic for "fifty"), blow for fifty-day periods at the end of April. It is generally best to avoid these windstorms by staying indoors when they blow particularly fiercely. Even so, no matter how well you seal the windows and doors, a fine layer of dust manages to seep in and settle on surfaces.

Average temperatures range between 57°F (14°C) in winter and 86°F (30°C) in summer. Extreme temperatures in the interior can drop to 44°F (7°C) in the winter and soar to 109°F (43°C) in the summer. Coastal areas may have the relief of summer breezes coming off the sea, but this comes at a cost—humidity that can be as debilitating as the scorching dry heat of the interior.

EGYPTIAN CITIES

Cairo, the vibrant capital of Egypt, is known as the "City of a Thousand Minarets." It is home to some of the world's most iconic landmarks, including the pyramids of Giza, the Sphinx, and the Egyptian Museum. Old and new coexist side by side—from cultural traditions to modes of transportation and architecture.

Luxor (historic Thebes), located on the banks of the Nile to the south, is steeped in ancient history. Visitors can explore the Valley of the Kings and Queens, where many pharaohs were buried, or visit the stunning temples of Karnak and Luxor.

Cairo's Historic District with the Sultan Hasan mosque in the foreground.

Aswan, the "Jewel of the Nile," is in southern Egypt. Visitors can take a boat to the temple complex on the island of Philae, or explore the colorful markets and bazaars.

Alexandria on the Mediterranean coast is a port city with a fascinating history and cultural heritage. Visitors can explore the ancient catacombs, visit the Bibliotheca Alexandria, or stroll along the city's waterfront promenade. It is renowned for its seafood.

Sharm El Sheikh, on the southern tip of the Sinai Peninsula, is a popular resort, famous for its beautiful beaches and clear blue waters, where visitors can go snorkeling or scuba diving to explore the coral reefs or take a camel ride in the nearby desert.

Whether you're interested in exploring ancient ruins, relaxing on beautiful beaches, or immersing yourself in local culture, Egypt's cities have something for everyone.

The harbor at Alexandria, near the Mamluk Citadel of Qaitbay.

THE PEOPLE

Egypt is the largest, most densely populated country in the Middle East/North Africa (MENA) region, with an estimated 113 million people. Most Egyptians are settled around the Nile, half of them in urban areas. Due to the rapid growth in population, towns and cities have burgeoned, consuming valuable agricultural land, and the economic and social demands of such a huge populace presents the government with many challenges.

Rural Egyptians are mainly engaged in agriculture, and villages are found around water sources, canals, and irrigation channels. An agrarian farmer is called a *fallah* (plural, *fellahin*). However, this term should be avoided by non-Egyptians who can't hope to understand the regional complexities associated with it—from it being socially acceptable to it being considered an insult, depending on who is saying it and to whom it is being said. Upper

Two farmers at harvest time in the Delta region.

Egyptians, who live south of Cairo around the Nile Valley, and who may also be engaged in the agricultural sector, are referred to as Sa'idi. Egypt's desert dwellers are the Bedouin, originally descended from Arab and Berber tribes. Nubian communities live in the far south.

In spite of their diversity, Egyptians are a relatively cohesive society, in which 90 percent of the population are Muslim—a religion that upholds communal unity.

Egyptian Identity

Although most of Egypt's land mass is situated on the African continent, the Egyptians do not identify as Africans in the same way as most inhabitants of other African countries do. Rather their self-image is shaped by their identification with Arab nationalism and Islam.

Throughout the period of Ottoman rule, both Ottomans and Europeans referred to the Arabic-speaking populations of subject nations such as Egypt and Sudan as "Arabs."

It was only after 1860, with the rise of Egyptian nationalism, that the state began to foster a collective Egyptian consciousness and sense of nationhood, in opposition to the de facto Anglo–French control.

Anger and disaffection with the pro-European regime of the Ottoman Khedive (viceroy) Tewfik Pasha ignited the Orabi Revolution of 1879–82. Led by Ahmed Orabi, an army officer and early Egyptian prime minister, the uprising called on people to reject imperial and colonially imposed definitions and to identify themselves as *masreyeen* (Egyptian). Campaigning under the slogan of "Egypt for Egyptians," the Orabi movement was the first major instance of Egyptian anticolonial nationalism.

Following the suppression of the Orabi revolt in 1882 and the British occupation of Egypt, Egyptian nationalists espoused an ethno-territorial secular form of nationalism that harked back to the legacy of Pharaonic culture—the pre-Christian and pre-Islamic civilization of Ancient Egypt.

"Pharaonism" became the dominant expression of national identity among anticolonial activists during the prewar and interwar periods. They rejected Arab nationalist sentiment, did not consider Egyptians to be part of the Arab nation, and did not regard Egypt as an Arab land. In 1918 the Egyptian nationalist leader Saad Zaghloul met with Arab delegates in Versailles and emphasized that their struggles were not connected—Egypt's problem was an Egyptian, not an Arab, one.

However, as other nations in the Arab world underwent similar independence struggles, pan-Arab–Islamic political sentiment in Egypt was kindled by the solidarity they felt with their regional neighbors, particularly with the rise of

Zionism in neighboring Palestine. These factors aroused the sympathies of King Farouk, the Egyptian prime minister Mustafa el-Nahhas, and Islamic movements such as the Muslim Brotherhood.

Until the 1940s, Egypt favored territorial Egyptian nationalism and distanced itself from pan-Arabism. However, Britain's reoccupation of Iraq in 1941—to prevent it from joining the Axis powers—provoked anger throughout the Arab world, and rising pan-Arab sentiment led to the formation of the Arab Union Club in Egypt in 1942 to promote stronger bonds between Egypt and the Arab world. The Egyptian prime minister, Mostafa el-Nahas, adopted their manifesto, and committed to championing Arab nations' rights and interests, and to explore the notion of Arab unity.

When Gamal Abd al-Nasser became president in 1954, he saw no conflict between Egyptian *wataniyya* (patriotism) and Arab *qawmiyya* (nationalism) as all the Arab states had experienced similar anti-imperialist struggles; he considered solidarity among them to be imperative for independence, and Arab nationalism became a state policy. In 1958 Egypt and Syria formed the United Arab Republic, which lasted until 1961. However, Egypt retained the name until 1971, when it adopted the current official name, the Arab Republic of Egypt.

Although Nasser's brand of Arabism was not deeply entrenched in Egyptian society, solidarity with the Arab world was, and Egypt saw itself as the leader of this larger cultural group. Nasser stressed both Egyptian sovereignty and leadership of the common Arab cause. His successor, Anwar el-Sadat (1970), asserted a more Egypt-centric orientation through his public policy, insofar as he welcomed foreign investment and by his peace initiative with Israel, reaffirming Saad Zaghloul's assertion that only Egypt and the Egyptians were his responsibility. However, despite Sadat's attempts to root out pan-Arab sentiment, and specifically because of his peace deal with Israel, which went against popular opinion, Arab nationalism in Egypt remained a strong force.

Sadat's successor, Hosni Mubarak, emphasized Pharaonism as the foundation of Egyptian identity. Rather than promoting pan-Arab solidarity he took a stand against terrorism, gaining him popularity in the West.

After the region-wide Arab Spring in 2011 and the revolution in Egypt that led to Mubarak's downfall, his brief successor, Mohamed Morsi, had his hands full internally and very little opportunity to involve himself in flare-ups in neighboring countries, and this was met by protestors supporting regional Arab solidarity, which was one of the factors that led to his demise.

Morsi's successor, President Abdel Fattah el-Sisi, has focused on developing the New Republic—basically a renaissance of the economy with innovation, education, and social justice. This is less concerned with questions of identity and more with infrastructural projects and investor relations (both regional and international).

Today, some Egyptians emphasize the connection between Egyptian and Arab identities, pointing to the central role that Egypt plays in the Arab world. Others, however, give greater weight to Egypt's ancient heritage, culture, and long existence as an independent state, and stress the failure of Arab and pan-Arab nationalist policies. While there is no firm consensus as to the nature of Egyptian identity, it is undisputed that Egypt retains its cultural ascendancy throughout the Arab world.

A BRIEF HISTORY

Egypt's culture has been influenced by contact over millennia with many very different societies and civilizations. Yet from ancient times to the present Egyptian society has been predominantly agricultural, and the Nile remains the bountiful provider in an otherwise barren desert. There is a link between the Egyptians of antiquity and their modern descendants, which finds an echo in persisting traditions and attitudes.

During its history, Egypt has often risen to greatness, dominating its neighbors culturally and politically; at other times it has been overshadowed by, if not subservient to, them. Yet, until recently, the country's productive lands have meant that, given the right conditions, the times of adversity have not lasted and Egypt has managed to reassume a leading cultural and political role. This frequent exchange of roles, from dominant empire to exploited dependency, is another important aspect of their history that affects the Egyptians' psyche, as they tend to consider it only a matter of time before Egypt resumes its leading role among the nations.

Ancient Egypt (6000 BCE–323 BCE)
Archaeological evidence shows that primitive farming began along the banks of the Nile at least as early as the

tenth millennium BCE. In around 8000 BCE, climatic changes desiccated large areas of North Africa, forcing groups of pastoralists to converge on the Nile Valley and stimulating the development of advanced agricultural communities. To this day Egyptians live along the Nile, separated from other population centers to the west and east by hundreds of miles of desert.

Around 6000 BCE the Egyptians were growing cereal crops and herding animals, constructing large buildings, and using metal tools. By 4000 BCE they were trading with neighboring lands and had developed proto-hieroglyphics. By the end of this millennium there were two separate states in Egypt—northern (Lower) Egypt and southern (Upper) Egypt. Around 3100 BCE Pharoah Narmer (or Menes), the ruler of Upper Egypt, conquered Lower Egypt, uniting Egypt for the first time, and he and his successors established the First Dynasty of Ancient Egypt.

Farmer plowing. Mural from the burial chamber of Sennedjem, circa 1200 BCE.

Pharaonic history is traditionally divided into thirty-one dynasties. Narmer's First Dynasty initiated Ancient Egyptian history, while the Thirty-First brought it to a close in 332 BCE, when Alexander the Great arrived in Egypt. Historians have combined groups of dynasties to define three Kingdoms: Old (Third to Sixth Dynasties), Middle (Eleventh to Thirteenth), and New (Eighteenth to Twentieth), as well as a Late Period (Twenty-Fifth to Thirty-First). Each of the three Kingdoms lasted for about four to five centuries. The pharaohs who ruled during these periods and the monuments they erected are those most familiar to us today.

The dynasties outside these three Kingdoms ruled mostly during times of civil war and disunity, or during partial or total foreign domination. Particularly after the end of the New Kingdom, several dynasties were foreign,

The Sphinx in front of the Great Pyramid of Giza.

and weak Egyptian rulers yielded control of Egypt to
Libyan, Nubian, Assyrian, and Persian dynasties.

Greco–Roman Egypt (332 BCE–330 CE)

Egypt became part of Alexander the Great's huge empire
in 332 BCE, and thus began almost a millennium of Greek
influence. On his death in 323 BCE , Alexander's empire,
which extended from Greece to northern India, began
crumbling. Egypt became the independent realm of
Alexander's close companion, the Macedonian general
Ptolemy, who declared himself king in 305 BCE , thus
founding the Ptolemaic dynasty and making Egypt an
imperial center once more.

Ptolemaic Egypt (323 BCE–30 BCE)

Although Alexander spent little time in Egypt before his
death, he laid the foundations for the city of Alexandria.
The Ptolemies made Alexandria their new capital, and for
centuries it was the greatest city of antiquity. Its famous
lighthouse on the island of Pharos was one of the Seven
Wonders of the Ancient World, while its magnificent
library was the first state-funded scientific institution,
attracting scholars from across the Hellenized world.

The Ptolemaic rulers adopted Egyptian customs and
dress, built temples for Egyptian gods, and took on the
role of the ancient pharaohs. Nevertheless, as thousands of
Greeks migrated to Egypt, a dual culture was established.
The rulers and the Greek immigrants, who enjoyed
special privileges, together with the wealthier Egyptian
classes, forged a Greco-Egyptian, Greek-speaking society.
Meanwhile, the bulk of the farming population, especially

in Upper Egypt, were left largely undisturbed. The pattern of a privileged foreign ruling class with an alien culture—remaining separate from the mass of the mainly agrarian population with its local language and customs—is one that was to repeat itself over the course of history as various overseas powers exchanged control of Egypt.

For much of the fourth and third centuries BCE, Ptolemaic Egypt was one of the most powerful states in the Eastern Mediterranean. Yet, by the second century BCE, it was weakened by internal instability as members of the dynasty fought each other for supremacy. By this time Rome was the dominant power in the Mediterranean.

The last Ptolemaic ruler, the famous Egyptian-born Cleopatra VII, became involved in Roman politics, first as Julius Caesar's lover, and then, after Caesar's assassination, as Mark Anthony's lover and ally in the continuing Roman civil war. They were defeated by the forces of Octavian, who became the first Roman emperor, Augustus. Cleopatra committed suicide and her son by Caesar was killed, thus ending Ptolemaic rule.

Bust of Cleopatra VII, Queen of Egypt.

Roman Egypt (*30 BCE–330 CE*)

Like the Ptolemies, Roman emperors appear in traditional pharaonic form on Egyptian temple walls. However, Egypt was now an imperial province and no longer the center of an empire; nevertheless it prospered under Roman rule, at least until the third century CE. Rome's primary interest in Egypt was its grain supply, but it was also an important base for trading with the East.

There was no large Roman population in Egypt and Latin was never adopted by the Egyptians. The Greek-speaking elite continued to dominate cultural life, while local culture remained alive in the countryside. Egyptian religious customs continued, and Egyptian temples remained in use.

Alexandria was surpassed in greatness by Rome but kept its position as the second city of the Mediterranean world. It remained the main center of Hellenistic learning and is today one of the world's oldest continuously occupied cities.

Christianity

The history of early Christianity has many links with Egypt. The Holy Family is believed to have sought sanctuary in Egypt during the infancy of Jesus. The first Egyptian Christians are believed to have been converted by Mark the Evangelist, who is therefore considered the first Egyptian patriarch (or pope). Alexandria hosted the very first Christian catechetical school. Celebrated Doctors of the Church, notably Origen, St. Athanasius, and St. Cyril of Alexandria, were Egyptians. It was in Egypt that both the Arian and Nestorian heresies were born. Many believe that the Christian symbol of the cross first came into use in Egypt and that it was partially derived from the Egyptian Ankh—the key of life.

Perhaps Egypt's most important contribution to Christianity was monasticism. This developed in the third century CE, when many Egyptian Christians, threatened by persecution, fled to the desert to establish new communities out of the state's reach. In the fourth century CE, Egyptians such as St. Anthony and Pachomius developed monastic rules and ideas, which spread to the rest of the Christian world.

Byzantine Rule (330–642)

Although Egyptian Christianity started in Alexandria, most converts were Egyptian rather than Greek, and by about 200 CE Christianity had spread throughout Egypt's towns and into rural areas. The scriptures were translated into the Greek-influenced Egyptian language used at the time, known today as Coptic, which remains the Egyptian Coptic Church's official language.

The Romans persecuted Christians until the end of the third century, but in the early fourth century Christianity became the official religion of the Byzantine Empire (as the later Roman Empire is called). The numbers of Christians increased greatly, as did hostility toward pagan forms of worship. In 391 CE, the Emperor Theodosius ordered all heathen temples destroyed, and paganism was outlawed throughout the Empire. Among the buildings destroyed by fire was the Library of Alexandria, a bastion of classical learning. Fanatical monks' attacks on pagan temples were recorded as late as the fifth century and it is unlikely that any pagans survived into the seventh century. Christianity extinguished the ancient religions, the roots of which went back to pharaonic Egypt. But Egyptian religious identity remained independent and expressed itself through the new faith.

The Coptic Church

In the two centuries following the Roman Empire's adoption of Christianity, the leading clergy, including Egyptian bishops, conducted doctrinal debates about the "nature" of Christ, which sometimes resulted in schisms that shaped the history of the Church.

Political maneuvering between the Alexandrian and Roman dioceses contributed to the outcome of the Council of Chalcedon in 451. This council repudiated the Monophysite doctrine associated with the Alexandrian Church—that in Christ there was but one nature—and removed the Alexandrian patriarch from office.

Most Egyptian clergymen and worshipers rejected this and reacted by appointing their own patriarch, so giving birth to a new Egyptian Church—the Coptic Church—independent of the bishops of Rome and Constantinople. For almost two centuries the Byzantine state put pressure on the Copts to renounce their "heresy." Torture and execution were sometimes used, causing great resentment of Byzantine rule, and the Coptic Church became the focus of Egyptian national identity.

Islamic Egypt

At the beginning of the seventh century a new religion was born in western Arabia that would change the world. By 634 the tribes of Arabia had united under the banner of this religion, Islam. Muslim Arab armies defeated the forces of Sassanid Persia and the Byzantine Empire, the two main powers of the region.

After ten years of conflict, most of the Middle East had fallen to Muslim forces. Within another decade the

Sassanid Empire was no more, and the Byzantines were confined to their territories in the Balkans, Greece, and Asia Minor. An Islamic empire had been created that, at its territorial peak in the early eighth century, stretched from the Atlantic to the Indian Ocean.

Province of the Caliphate (642–868)

After defeats in Syria in the mid-630s, the Byzantines were on the defensive. By 642, Egypt was fully occupied by the Muslims and became a province of the Caliphate, as the Muslim empire was known. The mostly Coptic Egyptian population were not sorry to see the Byzantines leave. Islamic law states that "People of the Book," that is, Jews and Christians, who live under Muslim rule must be protected and should not be harmed. Thus, the Muslims treated the local populations well, and they were rarely pressured to convert. In Egypt conversion to Islam was a slow process—it took about seven centuries for the Muslim population of Egypt to exceed the 50 percent mark.

As Alexandria was subject to Byzantine raids and was even briefly reoccupied in the 640s, the Muslims built a new capital inland, just south of the Delta. The new town, called al-Fustat, was also more accessible to reinforcements from Syria if required.

Egypt spent two centuries as a Muslim province, supplying the reigning caliphs with revenue from agricultural taxation. Arab tribes settled along the Nile Valley, and while their population was too small to affect the country's ethnic or religious composition, they were important in the adoption of the Arabic language.

Egyptian Muslim Empires

The caliphs were the Prophet Mohammed's political successors and they originally ruled from Medina in western Arabia. In 661 they were replaced by the Umayyad caliphs, who ruled from Damascus, and in 750 the Abbasids took over, ruling from their capital, Baghdad.

During its first two centuries, Islam divided into two main branches: Sunnism and Shi'ism. Shi'ism further split into different groups. Among them, the main group, the Imami, typically distanced itself from political activism, while the Isma'ili Shi'is were militantly anti-Abbasid, especially in the ninth century. The caliphs and the main political forces were Sunni, and easily kept the Shi'is and other political opponents in check. However, in the ninth century the Caliphate began to weaken, and the peripheries became detached.

As the Abbasid Caliphate weakened, Egypt gravitated toward political independence. Ibn Tulun, the Abbasid general sent to govern Egypt in 868, was independent of Baghdad in all but name. His armies kept the Caliphate's forces at bay, and he expanded Egyptian control into Palestine and Syria. The pattern was repeated by al-Ikhshid, who controlled Egypt from 935.

In the early tenth century a rebellion by Isma'ili Shi'is erupted in many of the Caliphate's provinces, where they managed to create scattered independent states. Egypt came under threat from one of these, created by a dynasty called the Fatimids, who were based in Mahdiya in modern-day Tunisia. They extended their control over most of North Africa and even proclaimed themselves caliphs in opposition to the Sunni Caliph in Baghdad.

The Fatimid Caliphate (969–1157)

In 969 the Fatimids invaded Egypt, and by 970 their armies had reached Syria, aiming to topple the Abbasid Caliphate in Baghdad. The Fatimid rulers decided to move their capital to Egypt, which was wealthy and closer to their enemies in Iraq, and they built a new city just north of the old Muslim capital of al-Fustat. The new capital was called *al-Qahira* (meaning "The Victorious"), better known in English as Cairo. Despite their early successes against the Abbasids, the Fatimids never managed to conquer Iraq, and spent a century fighting in northern Syria against the Abbasids and the Byzantines.

In the eleventh century, Turkish tribes from Central Asia broke through the Caliphate's weak eastern defenses. The Turks, newly converted to Islam, established a powerful Seljuk sultanate in the territories of the Abbasid Caliph, who became a political figurehead during their reign. They then attacked the Fatimids in Syria.

The Fatimids had created a powerful regional empire centered on Egypt, including much of North Africa, Syria, and western Arabia, and trading colonies in Yemen and western India. Their early rulers opened up trade routes to India and Egypt prospered. Cairo started to rival Baghdad in its splendor and prosperity: commerce and industry flourished, and it became an intellectual and artistic center.

Soon, however, the Fatimid state became embroiled in power struggles, and proved no match for the Christian armies of the First Crusade, which had conquered Syria and Palestine in 1098–9. The Crusaders repeatedly rebuffed the Fatimids' attempts to retake Palestine.

In the twelfth century, a small but powerful new Turkish

state established itself in inland Syria. Realizing Egypt's importance, the Crusaders and the Syrian Turks vied to control Egypt. The Turks eventually triumphed, and the tottering Fatimid Caliphate fell. The general commanding the Turkish forces in Egypt was a Kurd by the name of Salah al-Din, known in the West as Saladin.

The Ayyubids (1157–1250)

Empowered by Egypt's wealth, Saladin united Egypt and inland Syria before turning to deal with the Crusaders on the coast. In 1157, he destroyed their armies at Hattin near the Sea of Galilee and then captured Jerusalem. The Crusaders held on to isolated coastal cities, and the Third Crusade brought them a reprieve, but they were never again a power in the region.

Saladin established the Ayyubid sultanate, which continued to rule Egypt and Syria. He built the massive Cairo Citadel, which became Cairo's military headquarters and remained so until the twentieth century.

The pattern of power in the Ayyubid dynasty followed the Turkish model, which relied on a loose alliance between the ruling family's members and local tribal chiefs—in the Ayyubid case, Kurdish as well as minor Turkish leaders in Syria. This meant that the ruler lacked absolute power, had to rely on consensus, and had continuously to appease his many allies, resulting in an unstable political system. The Europeans realized that to control the Holy Land they first had to control prosperous and populous Egypt, and they duly dispatched fresh Crusades aimed at Egypt. Eventually, the internal instability of the Ayyubids and repeated Crusader attacks led the army to rebel against the Ayyubid sultan and, in 1250, to take power.

The Mamluks (1250–1517)

The last but one Ayyubid ruler had decided to build a new army loyal to himself alone, consisting mainly of Turkish slave soldiers called Mamluks (literally "owned" in Arabic). Slave soldiers had no legitimate way of ruling directly; in the past, even when powerful, they had at most managed to manipulate princes or caliphs and were united only along narrow factional lines. The Ayyubid Mamluks now faced the same problem and vied with each other for power.

However, events unfolded that would force them to unite. Pagan Mongols had broken through in the East and proceeded to decimate Iranian cities. In 1258 they reached Baghdad, destroyed the city, and executed the Abbasid Caliph. In 1259 they advanced into Syria. The Mamluk generals joined forces and faced the Mongols at Ain Jalut in Palestine, defeating them in a pitched battle. The Mongol tide had reached its limit, and the Mamluk sultans finally won legitimacy as the saviors of Islam.

The Mamluks almost immediately set about ridding the Levant of the other lingering enemy, the Crusaders. By 1291, Acre, in Palestine, the last major city held by the Crusaders, was captured and Egypt and Syria were united once more under the Mamluk sultans, ruling from Cairo.

The Mamluk state now became the center of Arab-Muslim culture. Iraq and nations to the east had fallen to the Mongols; the Mongol rulers over successor states there had converted to Islam but had adopted Persian or Turkish as their official language. With Baghdad destroyed, Cairo was now the first city of Islam, and the largest city in the fourteenth-century world.

Since the Crusades, the European demand for Eastern products, especially spices, had increased dramatically and the volume of this trade was huge and profitable. Egypt became a hub for trade between the East and the West, and its prosperity is reflected in the architectural heritage of Mamluk Cairo. In the fourteenth century, however, plague ravaged Egypt and Syria, there were a series of insufficient floods in Egypt, and in 1400 the Turco–Mongol warlord Tamerlane led a devastating invasion of Mamluk-controlled Syria, all of which led to famine and starvation in both countries. By the fifteenth century the Mamluk state was struggling economically and imposed higher taxes on international trade. As a result of the soaring prices of imported goods in Europe, Europeans began to invest in exploring alternative trade routes to the East.

The Rise of the Ottomans

In 1453 the Ottoman Turks captured Constantinople, finally destroying the ancient Byzantine Empire. Their armies controlled southeastern Europe and began strengthening their positions along the northern borders of Mamluk Syria.

In 1516, Ottoman forces entered Syria. The Mamluk troops were untrained, their generals were incompetent, and their failure to appreciate the latest advance in military technology (guns) saw them outmatched, and they were defeated. In 1517 the Ottoman army marched into Cairo and hanged the last Mamluk sultan from the city's gates.

Ottoman Province (1517–1805)

For the next three centuries Egypt was again an imperial dominion, and a prosperous one at that. Excess revenues were exported to the Ottoman capital of Istanbul (previously Constantinople), and skilled workers and artisans moved there. For the first time since the seventh century, the official language of the empire to which Egypt belonged was not Arabic, but Turkish.

By the eighteenth century, the Ottoman Empire had lost its place as a world power to the new European nation-states, and Egypt's governors pushed for more autonomy. In 1798, Europe, eager to get a slice of the Ottoman Empire, attempted to conquer some of its central lands.

The French Expedition to Egypt (1798–1801)

In 1798 Napoleon Bonaparte led an expedition to Egypt—seen as a halfway house to India—as part of the French Republic's campaign against the British Empire. The French army quickly occupied Egypt, but the invasion of Syria a year later failed, and in 1801 Ottoman and British forces eventually forced the French to withdraw. Despite the brevity of the French occupation, the event had significant repercussions. It opened the door for more European ventures into Ottoman territory, and it awakened the subjects of the Ottoman Empire, especially Egypt, to its lack of defenses against these advanced foreigners.

Egypt reverted to Ottoman control, but a power struggle ensued, with the population joining in. In 1805 Muhammad Ali, an Ottoman officer stationed in Egypt, supported by Egyptian religious and community leaders, imposed himself as governor of Egypt.

Napoleon's victory over the Ottomans at the Battle of Abukir, 1799.

The Dynasty of Muhammad Ali

With Muhammad Ali's rise to power (1805–48), Egypt entered its "modern period." Nominally an Ottoman governor, Muhammad Ali turned Egypt once again into an imperial center. He declared himself absolute ruler and removed political opponents and local threats, including the very local leaders who had helped bring him to power. He conscripted Egyptian farmers into a new, modern army and embarked on an ambitious program of industrialization based on the European model. This was the foundation on which the Egyptian Army was built. Officers, engineers, doctors, and technicians were trained in Europe, or locally by Europeans. Muhammad Ali's territorial ambitions led to expansion deep into Sudan, Syria, and western Arabia.

Portrait of Muhammad Ali Pasha, by August Couder.

By the 1820s Egypt was a formidable regional power. During conflict with the Ottoman sultan in the 1830s, Egyptian forces twice brought the Ottoman Empire to its knees, and only European intervention prevented them from marching into Istanbul. Finally, in 1841, Britain and other European powers forced Muhammad Ali to reduce the size of his forces and withdraw from Syria and Arabia. In exchange, the Ottomans granted his descendants hereditary "governorship" of Egypt and Sudan.

Under his successors, especially Isma'il Pasha (1863–79), modernization accelerated, particularly in education, agriculture, and communications. In 1854 Egypt built Africa's first railway line. The most spectacular infrastructural feat was the excavation of the Suez Canal, which took eleven years to construct. Opened in 1869, it greatly increased Egypt's strategic importance, though at an astronomical cost, both financially and in human life.

Isma'il undertook many large-scale projects, but his financial management was incompetent. Borrowing from

European creditors at exorbitant rates eventually led to financial crisis. As usual, the rural poor were the first to suffer as taxes were raised yet further and harsher tax-collection methods were implemented. Only six years after the opening of the Suez Canal, Egypt was forced to sell its shares in the company to Britain at a very low price. Despite all these measures, Egypt was declared bankrupt. In 1876 the major creditors, Britain and France, assumed financial, and effectively political, control of the country.

Isma'il Pasha was forced to abdicate, and his more pliable son, Tewfik (1879–92), replaced him. The situation became intolerable for many Egyptians, and, as we have seen, in 1881 Ahmed Orabi led a successful uprising against the government, forcing Tewfik to concede reforms along nationalist lines. Threatened by this movement, the British landed troops in Alexandria in 1882 and suppressed the national revolt, and Egypt lost its independence once again.

The British Occupation

Although nominally an autonomous province of the Ottoman Empire, de facto Egypt was ruled by Britain from 1882. At the outbreak of the First World War in 1914, Egypt was declared independent of the Ottomans and became a British Protectorate, thus formalizing the British presence. The Protectorate ended in 1922 and Egypt was proclaimed a parliamentary monarchy. Despite gaining formal independence, Egypt was strategically important to the British Empire and Britain remained in control politically and militarily until after the Second World War.

During this period, much of the population supported the Wafd Party, established in 1919, which sought complete British withdrawal from Egypt. For thirty years, Egyptian politics was tri-polar—the king wanted more independence from the British, yet a tame parliament; the Wafd, representing the bulk of the people, was critical of both the king and the British; and the British used political and military pressure to contain any serious threat to their continued presence in the land.

The period gave rise to movements that persist until today, whether Islamic, Egyptian nationalist, or, a little later, Arab nationalist. Among these movements was the Islamist Muslim Brotherhood, established in 1927, as well as a revolutionary organization within the army known as the Free Officers, in the late 1940s.

Gamal Abd al-Nasser (1952–70)

Growing resentment of Britain's continued presence after the Second World War, defeat at the hands of the new Israeli state in 1948, and the political and moral corruption of the Egyptian monarch Farouk I (1936–52) led to a military coup by the Free Officers movement, driven by Colonel Gamal Abd al-Nasser.

In 1953, the Free Officers abolished the monarchy and elected General Mohamed Naguib as president. However, he was unwilling to enforce the sweeping political changes that they wanted, such as abolishing the parliamentary system, and he was removed from power in 1954. Nasser succeeded him as Egypt's second president.

Apart from Naguib, Nasser was the first ethnic Egyptian to rule Egypt since pharaonic times, and it was a matter of national pride to him that Egypt regain its lost grandeur. The first step was to remove the remaining British presence, and he negotiated a treaty according to which British troops would leave the Suez Canal zone in 1956.

Nasser envisaged an ambitious program of industrialization and modernization that would transform Egypt. A dam on the Nile at Aswan would generate power for new factories and protect agriculture from the occasionally destructive Nile floods. He first approached Britain and the USA for financial backing, but they declined to support him so he turned to the Soviet bloc. The Soviets, who were looking for new regional allies, duly offered financial support and industrial expertise.

While the Free Officers were not strictly socialist, Nasser's new regime became so. Property laws were passed that confiscated land from the huge estates of the land-owning class created by Muhammad Ali's dynasty and redistributed it among the peasants. The economy was closed off, and salaries and property rents were frozen, resulting in most of the large foreign community that ran Egypt's private enterprises leaving the country.

Suez

In 1956, Nasser nationalized the Suez Canal Company, which owned and controlled the canal. The British and French governments, who were the majority shareholders, were outraged by this move and decided to invade. They colluded in the Israeli invasion of Sinai and used the ensuing war as a pretext to occupy the Canal zone. But the USA and the Soviet Union opposed this operation and put political pressure on Britain and France, forcing

President Nasser in 1962.

them and the Israelis to withdraw. The outcome was an immense political victory for Nasser and dealt a severe blow to the prestige and power of the old colonial powers.

The victory of 1956 emboldened Nasser, who became a bitter enemy of Western imperialism and supported many African countries in their struggles for independence. Together with leaders such as Jawarhalal Nehru of India and President Tito of Yugoslavia, he formed the Non-aligned Movement to create an independent bloc—neither Soviet nor Western—to protect the Third World's interests.

Nasser also became the main champion of Arab nationalism, which called for a Pan-Arab state uniting the Arabic-speaking peoples. A product of this vision was the short-lived union between Egypt and Syria, the United Arab Republic (UAR), from 1959 to 1961.

The newly created state of Israel was seen as the main obstacle to Arab nationalism, as it had been established on the land of the Palestinian Arabs, of whom around 700,000 had become refugees.

This combination of positions bolstered Nasser's international image as the developing world's hero, but it made him enemies in the West. The USA, fearing the threat to its regional interests, increased its support of Israel and sought opportunities to curb Nasser's power. This would eventually lead to disaster for Egypt, and for the Palestinians whose cause he championed.

The '67 War

Disaster struck in 1967 when Israel, supported by the Western powers, launched an all-out offensive against the Egyptians, Jordanians, and Syrians. Taken by surprise, the Arab air forces were virtually wiped out on the ground, and Israel then easily occupied the remaining Palestinian land (the West Bank and Gaza), as well as taking Sinai from Egypt and the Golan Heights from Syria.

This was not only a military defeat, but a crippling blow to both Egypt's economy and its political prestige. The Suez Canal became the front line and was closed to shipping. Nasser died three years later, and it was left to his successor, Anwar al-Sadat, to try to sort out the mess.

Nasser has been criticized for being a dictator, for his socialist economic policies, and mostly for the disastrous 1967 defeat. Nevertheless, achievements such as nationalizing the Suez Canal, the construction of the Aswan Dam, land reforms that benefited most of the destitute peasantry, and massive industrial expansion ensured that almost five million mourners attended his funeral procession, one of the largest in history.

Anwar al-Sadat (1970–81)

In 1970, the vice president, Anwar al-Sadat, assumed power as president after Nasser's death. He attempted to reach a settlement with the Israelis to ensure the return of territories lost in the 1967 War. In response to the UN's Jarring Mission report, proposing a return to the pre-1967 borders in exchange for peace, Sadat declared that, if Israel agreed to withdraw from Sinai and the Gaza Strip and to implement other provisions stipulated in the report, Egypt would "be ready to enter into a peace agreement with Israel."

Israel refused to return to the pre-1967 lines, and in October 1973 the Egyptians and their Syrian allies launched a coordinated offensive against it. Unprepared, the Israelis suffered heavy casualties and faced defeat, but they managed to regain the initiative on both fronts, defeating the Syrians in the north and encircling half of the Egyptian forces in Sinai.

Politically, however, Sadat had achieved his objective and brought the Israelis to the negotiating table. His symbolic visit to Israel in 1977 resulted in a peace treaty between Egypt and Israel in 1979 and saw the Sinai Peninsula returned to Egypt. Other Arab states regarded this as a betrayal of their joint cause, and Egypt was ostracized; many Egyptians shared this feeling.

Economically, Sadat systematically reversed Nasser's socialist policies, implementing an Open Door Policy, lifting constraints on imports and foreign investment. These policies benefited many in the middle classes, and a new business class emerged. But government corruption increased, and basic commodity prices soared, affecting the poor majority. An attempt to remove bread subsidies in 1977 resulted in riots on an unprecedented scale. Economic hardship and a clampdown on the active socialist movement boosted the cause of Islamic radicals, whose numbers began to swell. In 1981, Sadat was assassinated by radical Islamists while attending an annual military parade celebrating the campaigns of the 1973 War.

Sadat is remembered variously by Egyptians. Many have a very high opinion of him and consider the 1973 War to have been an all-out victory over Israel that avenged Egypt's 1967 defeat. Peace with Israel ended a costly state of war and saw the return of Sinai. The liberalization of the economy benefited many. For others, Nasser's defiant foreign policy and economic socialism were correct, and they consider them to have been betrayed by Sadat. It is still common to hear Sadatists and Nasserists loudly arguing the merits of their favored leader in both working-class cafés and middle-class homes.

Hosni Mubarak (1981–2011)

Following Sadat's assassination, the vice president, General Hosni Mubarak, assumed power. He managed simultaneously to repair relations with the rest of the Arab world and to maintain Egypt's peace treaty with Israel. Unlike his predecessors, he refrained from taking major political risks and avoided foreign military entanglements.

Despite these diplomatic feats, Mubarak faced an Islamic fundamentalist terror campaign in the early 1990s. This targeted both tourists and the police force and took several years to subdue, during which time the police used heavy-handed tactics, especially in the south. Further liberalization of the economy created a boom in the late 1990s, but this growth almost ground to a halt in the first years of the new millennium.

In 2005, Mubarak launched a series of political reforms, culminating in Egypt's first-ever presidential elections, which took place later that year, and which he won resoundingly. In the following parliamentary elections, many members of the officially banned Muslim Brotherhood won seats by running as independent candidates. But political opponents continued to criticize the many restrictions that remained, considering the increase in freedoms to be far from secure. The growing internal opposition from different points on the political spectrum—including Islamists, liberals, and leftists, all calling for true democracy and greater political reform—regarded the reforms as cosmetic and aimed solely at easing a transfer of power within the regime.

The continued poverty, corruption, and culture of police abuse with impunity led to a series of daring demonstrations against the regime in 2004 and 2005 that planted the seeds of the popular uprising that would end Mubarak's rule in 2011.

TAHRIR SQUARE AND BEYOND

Mubarak enjoyed thirty years of near absolute power, marked by corruption and a strong security state. The regime had regularly justified its iron rule by the need to maintain stability. But—inspired by a popular uprising in Tunisia in December 2010—on January 25, 2011, hundreds of thousands of Egyptians took to the streets in a series of electrifying demonstrations demanding political and economic reforms and the overthrow of the regime.

Shortly after the ousting of Tunisian president Zine El Abidine Ben Ali, Egyptian political activists called for a day of nationwide protests on January 25—cleverly timed to coincide with a public holiday marking Police Day. The activists used social networking sites such as Facebook and Twitter to spread the news. The turnout on the day astounded even them, and security forces were deployed across the country to quell the protests.

Tahrir (the Arabic word for "freedom") Square, situated in the heart of Cairo, and long considered little more than a clogged traffic artery to be avoided during rush hour, was transformed into the symbolic heart of the Egyptian revolt, the flagship of the Arab Spring uprisings. After vicious street battles the police were overwhelmed, and the protesters took control of Tahrir Square.

On January 28, Mubarak ordered the army onto the streets. The army, which at the time enjoyed a good reputation, was widely welcomed by the protesters.

Perhaps realizing that his days were numbered, Mubarak attempted a series of desperate reforms, including a government reshuffle, appointing a vice president—his spymaster of twenty years, Omar Suleiman—engaging in national dialogue with opposition groups, and reassuring Egyptians that he would not seek reelection when his term ended in September 2011.

But his conciliatory measures, delivered in tense televised addresses, did not sway the protesters, who braved bullets, water cannons, and tear gas for eighteen days in a determined bid to bring down the regime.

Mubarak resigned on February 11 and handed power to a military council, the Supreme Council of the Armed

Forces (SCAF), headed by his longtime defense minister, Field Marshal Hussein Tantawi.

Following a series of protests demanding justice for the hundreds who had died during the revolt, Mubarak was jailed and put on trial for his involvement in the killings and for corruption—the first Arab dictator toppled by the Arab Spring revolts to appear in court.

On June 2, 2012, Mubarak was sentenced to life in prison for his role in the killing of protesters. He was acquitted in a separate corruption case along with his two influential sons, Alaa and Gamal. Dozens of former ministers, officials, and businessmen associated with his regime were also put on trial on various corruption charges, but the speedy nature of the process was criticized as politically motivated.

Military Rule

After Mubarak was toppled the SCAF was left in charge of the country. On taking power, it suspended the constitution, dissolved parliament, and promised to oversee a transitional phase that would pave the way for elections that would express the will of the people. It issued a constitutional declaration to serve as a temporary charter until a new constitution was drafted.

In November 2011, elections were held for the upper and lower houses of parliament, and previously banned Islamist movements, such as the powerful Muslim Brotherhood and more conservative groups representing the Salafi brand of Islam, won a crushing victory.

In 2012, the newly elected parliament was asked to elect members of a constituent assembly to draft the country's new constitution. But the assembly's overwhelmingly Islamist majority sparked furious demands by the secular parties for its dissolution, fearful that their goal of a civil state would be blocked by an Islamist political monopoly. A court dissolved the constituent assembly just weeks prior to presidential elections, and a new assembly was eventually appointed.

The military-led transition was divisive and tumultuous. The army's crackdown on dissent soon echoed Mubarak's tactics, prompting violent and sometimes deadly protests. Month after month, anti-military demonstrators took to the streets to demand the end of military trial of civilians, torture, censorship, forced "virginity tests" for female protesters, and acts of violence by the security forces.

Egypt's first free presidential elections were held on May 23 and 24, 2012. More than 50 million eligible voters were called to elect one of the twelve candidates vying to succeed Mubarak. Islamists, liberals, and leftists all promised radically different futures for the country.

With no outright winner, the election commission declared a second round of voting between the top two candidates—the Muslim Brotherhood's Mohamed Morsi and Mubarak's last prime minister, Ahmed Shafiq, a former air force commander.

The race had polarized the country, dividing those who feared a return to the old regime under Shafiq from those who wanted to keep religion out of politics and who feared the Brotherhood would stifle personal freedoms.

On the eve of the results, the SCAF issued a new constitutional declaration granting the army sweeping powers and paving the way for a power struggle with the future president.

Mohamed Morsi

In June 2012, Mohamed Morsi was declared president, narrowly beating Shafiq to become the first Islamist president of the Arab world's most populous nation. On July 10, 2012, he reinstated the Islamist-dominated parliament disbanded the previous month by the Supreme Constitutional Court and ordered the return of legislators elected in 2011, most of whom were members of his Freedom and Justice Party and other Islamist groups.

Morsi's later decisions went against the SCAF, which has historically held significant power and influence in Egypt. In August 2012, he asked Tantawi, head of the armed forces, and Sami Hafez Anan, the army chief of staff, to resign, and he fired two more high-ranking security officials, including the director of the Intelligence Directorate and the commander of the presidential guard. He appointed Abdel Fattah el-Sisi, the chief of military intelligence, as the new defense minister.

The new culture minister, Alaa Abdelaziz, fired the head of the Egyptian General Book Authority and the head of the Fine Arts Council, and dismissed Ines Abdel-Dayem, director of Cairo Opera, prompting prominent composer and musical director Nayer Nagui to accuse the government of having a "detailed plan to destroy culture and the fine arts in Egypt." Due to the persistent culture war between Islamists and liberals, Morsi was unable to secure the support of liberals and minorities.

In November 2012, Morsi issued a controversial declaration, announcing himself as sovereign head of the state, who could "claim exception against all rules." Egypt's highest body of judges denounced the decree as an "unprecedented assault on the independence of the judiciary and its rulings."

Protests against Morsi and the Muslim Brotherhood began later that month and continued into December, resulting in protestors gathering outside the presidential palace in Heliopolis and demanding that Morsi step down. Morsi accused the opposition parties of inciting violence and imposed a curfew when the protests spread, and on December 6, 2012, approximately seven people were killed and more than 600 wounded in clashes between Muslim Brotherhood supporters and the protestors.

Demonstrations continued until June 2013 and the Tamarod ("rebellion") movement collected allegedly more than 20 million signatures demanding Morsi's resignation and calling for mass protests to continue.

On June 26, 2013, Morsi tried to reconcile with the opposition, but he was accused of dismissing its concerns. Less than a week later, millions protested across the country demanding his resignation. The following day, the Egyptian Armed Forces issued a 48-hour ultimatum giving the country's political parties until July 3, 2013 to meet the Egyptian people's demands. The military removed Morsi from office and appointed Adly Mansour, the head of the Constitutional Court, as the interim president of Egypt.

Abdel Fattah el-Sisi

After the turmoil of the 2011 Revolution and Morsi's ineffective presidency, the Egyptians pinned their hopes on Morsi's minister of defense, Abdel Fattah el-Sisi, who in July 2013 had cracked down on the militant Islamic group Isis. El-Sisi leveraged his popularity by resigning and announcing his candidacy for the presidency. He was duly elected president in May 2014. He restored stability by improving the infrastructure, making economic reforms, and investing in the economy, thereby increasing a sense of optimism. He subsequently won the 2018 presidential election and his second term saw impressive cultural infrastructure projects such as the building of the city of New Cairo and the Grand Egyptian Museum.

El-Sisi continued to engage with international bodies, and in July 2022 he conducted a national dialogue with representatives from both liberal and Islamist groups to set a course for economic recovery. However, despite his promise to improve the quality of life for all, the removal of subsidies for basic foodstuffs, the unstable state of the economy, the lack of access to former markets affected by the Ukraine–Russia war, and a significantly devalued EGP after the Covid-19 pandemic created even more difficult circumstances for the poor in Egypt.

GOVERNMENT AND POLITICS

Since the time of President Mubarak, Egypt has had the structural attributes of a democratic government: a constitution, three separate branches of government, and a multiparty system. But much of the power rests in the executive branch. Egypt has been in a state of emergency almost continuously between 1967 and 2023 via a law that gives extra powers to the executive, limits nongovernmental political activity, and imposes restrictions on freedom of speech in the name of national security. The emergency law expired on May 31, 2012, but was renewed on August 14, 2013, when 149 protestors demanded Morsi's reinstatement. It was renewed by Sisi upon its expiration on October 26, 2021.

The Egyptian constitution proclaims the Arab Republic of Egypt to be a democratic state with Islam as its religion and Arabic as its national language. The president is the head of state and, together with the cabinet, constitutes the executive authority. Legislative power resides in the House of Representatives, which ratifies laws and examines and approves the budget. The judiciary includes secular and religious courts. The Senate was inaugurated in October 2020 after constitutional amendments reestablished an upper chamber.

Foreign Relations

For decades Egypt, a key mediator in the Middle East, has actively participated in regional negotiations and diplomatic efforts. It has had bilateral relations with Israel since the Camp David treaty of 1979 and is on friendly terms with the USA and major European countries, and with China and Russia. It also enjoys good relations with the UN, the Arab League, and the African Union, working toward regional cooperation and stability.

THE ECONOMY

Nasser's economic policy had been shaped by import substitution, agricultural reform, and industrialization. Government investment was at the top of the agenda, and until 1970 most sectors of the economy were state owned. Sadat's "Open Door Policy" changed the landscape.

Later economic reforms, in 1991, reduced tariffs and customs duties in order to continue the drive toward a market economy. New monetary policies reduced inflation and decreased the budget deficit, and a privatization program was launched. In 2004, the prime minister, Ahmed Nazif, introduced pro-business legislation and trimmed bureaucratic procedures to help encourage private and foreign investment. Egypt has been a member of the International Monetary Fund since 1945.

Since the 2007–2008 global financial crisis and the 2011 Revolution, however, Egypt has struggled to maintain economic stability. Mubarak's insertion of the military into economic sectors has been ramped up by Sisi. The coronavirus pandemic of 2019–21 and the attendant international lockdown led to steep inflation and a significant devaluation of the Egyptian pound.

Despite the rise in infrastructure expenditure, Egypt is still considered a poor country, and the various economic reforms and subsidy changes have had a major impact on the daily lives of ordinary people. In 2019, as part of a broader reform program, there were cuts to fuel subsidies, increases in electricity prices, and a 25 percent rise in the price of subsidized bread. In 2020, the government announced that it would gradually reduce fuel subsidies over three years. It raised electricity prices for households by an average of 19.5 percent, and raised the prices of some food products, including sugar and cooking oil, to reduce the burden on the state budget.

Meanwhile, overpopulation is putting a great strain on land and water resources. Unemployment among the young is rising, many professionals have become economic migrants, and the economy relies not only on remittances from overseas workers but also on foreign aid. Egypt is the fourth-largest recipient of aid from the USA.

Industry

Egypt's industry is dominated by iron and steel, textiles, chemicals, cement, sugar, and cotton, and there are major manufacturing plants in Cairo, Alexandria, Port Said, and Suez. The country has substantial energy reserves, both in traditional fossil fuels and in renewable energy. It produces a significant amount of petroleum, though this is small by Middle Eastern standards, and there are natural gas deposits at four sites in the Mediterranean. The most important of these is the giant Zohr Field, approximately 118 miles (190 km) north of Port Said, which is the largest-ever gas discovery to date in Egypt and the Mediterranean Sea.

Minerals found in Egypt are phosphates, salt, iron ore, manganese, limestone, gypsum, and gold.

Agriculture

Egypt's farmland is heavily cultivated, and agriculture accounts for about 11.3 percent of the GNP. The Aswan Dam, completed in 1970, was built to control the annual floods and to generate electricity, and has made more land available for agriculture, but it has also reduced the amount of nutrient-rich silt coming from Upper Egypt.

A large percentage of the labor force is engaged in agriculture. The main crop is cotton, followed by maize, wheat, broad beans, sugar cane, onions, rice, potatoes, and citrus fruit, and Egypt imported approximately half its food prior to the 2022 policy changes governing importation.

To manage the economy sustainably and responsibly after the Covid-19 pandemic, Sisi reduced imports by almost US $1.5 billion to essential items such as chemical and mineral products, transportation equipment, foodstuffs, and consumer goods, and today Egypt's main import partners are Germany, Italy, China, Turkey, Saudi Arabia, Kuwait, Lebanon, the US, and India.

Exports account for about 25 percent of GDP. The major exports are oil and other mineral products, chemical products, agricultural products, livestock and animal fats, and textiles (mainly cotton). Other exports include base metals, machinery and electrical appliances, foodstuffs, beverages, and tobacco. Egypt's major export partners are Italy, Spain, France, Saudi Arabia, India, and Turkey. Others include the US, Brazil, and Argentina.

Tourism

Tourism is a pillar of the economy, generating about 10.7 percent of Egypt's foreign currency revenue and accounting for approximately 12 percent of GDP. In the 1990s terrorist threats had a negative effect on the tourist industry, but Mubarak's government put in place strong counter-insurgency policies and Sisi has maintained these and invested further in infrastructure.

The 2011 Revolution and later the Covid-19 pandemic brought tourism to a halt, but the sector has seen some recovery in its efforts to attract foreign visitors, particularly in Cairo and in mainland Egypt. Tourism in the Red Sea resorts has always fared well.

During Morsi's brief reign, Islamist rule raised questions about the tourist industry's future, particularly beach tourism, which some feared would be affected by the application of a strict interpretation of Islamic law. However, this did not materialize and the concerns proved groundless. Nevertheless, while foreign visitors can comfortably enjoy Egypt's beautiful beaches in Western swimwear, they should remember to maintain a respectful modesty in areas not frequented by tourists.

The Sinai Peninsula has seen a spike in security-related problems since the 2011 Revolution. The northern part of the peninsula has been the base of an army campaign aimed at rooting out Islamist militants responsible for attacks on gas pipelines and security installations.

The southern part of Sinai has been less affected, and tourists continue to flock to the luxury Red Sea resorts. Security across the country is typically visible; however, this region in particular is more heavily guarded, and travelers can expect to encounter checkpoints in remote areas. It is advisable for travelers to always keep their passports on them.

CHAPTER TWO

VALUES &
ATTITUDES

Egyptian culture and attitudes are shaped by the deeply rooted customs of an ancient civilization and the "Egyptianizing" of other cultural traditions. Additionally, the Nile Valley, or *Sa'id*, (in the south of the country) and the Delta (in the north) vary considerably, with the Sa'id being typically more conservative and religious.

Modern Egyptians are, of course, concerned with much the same issues as people anywhere else in the world. Urban, educated Egyptians are well informed and smart. Typically, the first question they will ask a visitor is "Where are you from?" as they are keen to make you feel at ease, and eager to show off their knowledge of different parts of the world.

Because Egypt is such a significant tourist destination, Egyptians interact with people from all over the world, and in the main cities they are generally able to converse with travelers. Many educated urbanites are polyglot, not only picking up the basics of foreign languages, but mastering them. However, not everyone speaks English, so rather than expect them to, it would be a nice gesture to try and learn some basic words of Arabic. Sometimes, when Egyptians are approached in a foreign language they do not understand, they may not respond. This is often misconstrued as unfriendliness, which is highly unlikely as Egyptians are innately hospitable and will do their utmost to make anyone, including foreigners, feel at home. In such a case it would be best to try to illustrate what you want to know, or smile, move on, and ask someone else. The perceived rudeness is not intentional; it's usually just a reluctance to engage due to shyness.

Obliging Nature

When Egyptians are asked for something, they feel a sense of duty to try to oblige. They will make a real effort not to refuse a request directly, and to suppress irritation or annoyance. If asked directions in the street, and an Egyptian doesn't know the answer, they will often rather guess than say they can't help, even if it would actually have been more helpful to simply say, "I don't know." Promises are made easily, though not always fulfilled, which could well be because they don't like to disappoint and would rather agree to someone's request than let them down.

Time Observance

The day-to-day running of affairs may sometimes seem haphazard and random. Appointments and commitments are usually honored, but this does vary, and patience should be practiced. The increasing traffic congestion in the major metropolises is usually the reason for lateness. Being late for an appointment is not the end of the world, nor does it mean the end of a business deal.

By and large, the Egyptians are friendly, cheerful, hospitable, and renowned for their sense of humor. Most of them endure difficult living conditions daily. Many need to juggle several jobs to earn a decent income, but despite this they seem to accept their lot with little fuss. They are considerably and visibly more religious than Westerners, and believe in the concept of an afterlife, working hard in this life and hoping to reap the benefits in the next. They deal with problems by saying *insha'Allah* (it is the will of Allah)—a term often heard. This calmness, sometimes interpreted as indifference, is merely a survival tactic.

That is not to say that the Egyptians are docile. While they will make great efforts to maintain someone else's dignity, if they feel insulted tempers will flare. For example, if a man's wife has been harassed, he cannot ignore it, and may well get into a fistfight over the issue. If slighted in a traffic altercation, the two drivers may well holler and get into an aggressive, but non-physical, argument in order to restore their pride. Egyptians can be quite loud in certain areas, and many visitors have been alarmed to see people bellowing at each other, only to discover that it's not an argument at all, just a boisterous exchange.

THE CONCEPT OF *MAAT*

The Ancient Egyptian goddess Maat, daughter of the Sun god Re, was the personification of truth, justice, and cosmic order. The principles she embodied—of balance, harmony, morality, and law—underpinned social interaction and were core concepts of Ancient Egyptian religion and ethics. Traces of *Maat* are still evident today.

The concept of *Maat* covers three aspects: acting for each other, speaking and listening to each other, and thinking of each other. In that sense it can be seen as the forerunner of the solidarity and social justice at the heart of contemporary Egyptian culture, where the group's needs take precedence. The emphasis is on order and social harmony, and familial and social relationships and bonds are prioritized over individual wants and needs.

These underlying values are generally consistent across class and country, and in any dealings with an Egyptian it is essential to start from a base of respect. Communication should be conducted with politeness, to accord *sharaf* (honor) to others, the guiding principle of behavior and social interaction. Honor is deeply connected to an Egyptian's *karama* (personal dignity). Egyptians demonstrate their honor and dignity in their loyalty to their family, their helpfulness toward others, their charitability, how they dress, their manner of presentation, respect toward authority and their elders, and the hospitality they extend to friends and visitors.

STATUS AND SOCIAL STRUCTURE

From the 1940s until the Revolution of 1952, population growth, the spread of education, industrialization, and the migration from rural to urban areas drove a degree of social mobility. Despite this, there was a clear division between the wealthy landowning class and the agricultural workers, as well as a relatively new working class recruited from the farmers.

The 1952 Revolution paved the way for drastic changes to the class system. The new socialist ideology meant that crossing class barriers was no longer an impossible goal. Two main ways to achieve upward mobility included a good education, or a career in the army. The professional middle class expanded, and an industrial working class came into being during Nasser's tenure. The post 1952 Revolution years also gave rise to a new military class. Eventually, status was no longer associated with wealth and land but with power and connections to the regime.

After Nasser's death in 1970, Sadat replaced the socialist economic system with laissez-faire capitalism. His market-directed "Open Door Policy" enabled many entrepreneurs and opportunists to make money and paved the way for the growth of a new wealthy middle class.

Upward mobility continues to this day and consequently the class structure is ambiguous. Today Egyptian society is loosely divided into three groups: an extremely wealthy class that is powerful through connections and money; most Egyptians, who are extremely poor; and a small professional and middle class, which is educated. While the class system is not as institutionalized as it is in other parts of the world, Egyptian society is very class-based. People instinctively work and socialize within their own class. Social gaps exist between rich and poor, educated and illiterate, urban and rural.

The wealthy have adopted many of the values of Western society; they dress and behave in a similar fashion. They carry laptops and iPods, and wear designer clothes. The rest of society is largely conservative; it holds to traditional values, where family and religion play central roles. The small middle and professional class typically stands between aspiring to the ostentatious consumerism of the wealthy—by buying cheap copies of expensive branded clothing and accessories—and maintaining their religion and traces of conservatism.

Another clear division is the urban–rural divide. Many upper-class urbanites still regard rural people as backward. In their vocabulary the word *fallah* (peasant) is derogatory, and they make no attempt to hide their privilege; indeed it is acceptable to flaunt designer wear and expensive accessories. Meanwhile, some country townsfolk think that urbanites have loose morals and consider them degenerate. In the countryside the class structure is similar.

While old family names still matter in the villages, as they do in the cities, status relates to power. Those with family or social ties to the regime enjoy significantly more power and privileges than those who do not.

HONOR AND REPUTATION

It can be somewhat disconcerting for foreigners when they encounter Egyptians who stress their positive qualities or emphasize their family's achievements. This may seem immodest and egotistical to an outsider; however, a family's name and honor is important to Egyptians, and any blight on the family's name or honor is shameful, so Egyptians typically feel it necessary to assert their family's and by extension their own honorable reputation.

Being a *Muwazzaf*

Nasser instituted a system whereby university graduates were guaranteed jobs for life in the public sector. Being a *muwazzaf* (government employee) is a status symbol— a lifelong job with a pension and benefits, which allow people to secure credit or buy items payable in installments and enjoy artificially raised living standards. But the growing population caused problems for the government, which had to find employment for graduates when vacancies no longer existed. As a result, the public sector became bloated, and several people were hired to perform the work of one person. Today the desire for the title of *muwazzaf* still exists, particularly in rural Egypt, even though the government can no longer guarantee a job. While the young may desire a cushy government job, they no longer turn down other work, and tend to move to major cities to seek better opportunities. Those with the means go abroad, and those without education or the means travel to the main tourist centers. Of course, there are those who aren't capable of either and they contribute to the ranks of the unemployed.

EGYPTIAN PRIDE

Egypt's contribution to science and technology is generally associated with its ancient and medieval past, but Egyptian invention and innovation in many fields has continued uninterrupted. There are many notable contemporary Egyptian pioneers in science, art, religion, astronomy, and language, among other disciplines.

Historically, Egypt's central position in the Middle East established it as a channel of knowledge between Europe, Africa, and the Middle East. Scholars at the Library of Alexandria, built in the Ptolemaic era (c. 300 BCE), transcribed and shared information, making significant contributions to science, astronomy, mathematics, and medicine. Al-Azhar University was established in the tenth century and contributed to the spread of knowledge. Today it continues to inform dialogue in religious and philosophical matters. In the tenth century Ibn al-Haytham developed the science of optics, and in the thirteenth century Ibn al-Nafis posited the pulmonary circulation of blood in the body.

In the twentieth century Dr Sameera Moussa (1917–52) became known as "the Mother of Atomic Energy" for her work in developing the equation that broke down the atoms of cheap metals, such as copper, enabling the development of cheaper nuclear technology. Ahmed Zewail (1946–2016), "the Father of Femtochemistry," was the first Egyptian to receive a Nobel Prize for his contribution to femtochemistry (the study of chemical reactions in extremely short timescales). Dr Hatem Zaghloul (1957–) developed technologies that were the forerunners of the internet and Wi-Fi, building on Hedy Lamarr's frequency-hopping communication technology. Other Nobel Prize winners are Anwar Sadat (Peace Prize, 1978), Naguib Mahfouz (Literature, 1988), Ahmed Zewail (Chemistry, 1999), and Mohamed ElBaradei (Peace Prize, 2005).

Egypt was industrialized in the nineteenth century, well ahead of other Arab countries, and the population constitutes almost a quarter of all the Arabs. Egyptians are extremely proud of their heritage and of their position as cultural and political leaders in the Arab world. However, they are well aware of their social problems. Rampant poverty, overcrowding, and continued unemployment make life difficult for the great majority. This information may not be readily admitted to or shared with foreigners as Egyptians feel honor-bound to portray the positive side of their country. Speaking negatively about your country in front of a foreigner is equivalent to washing your dirty linen in public. Two Egyptians having coffee together might criticize their society or government but, as soon as a foreigner walks in, they will stop. In fact, if a foreigner wants to hear an Egyptian's honest opinion of Egypt, he or she must compliment the place.

SOCIAL NETWORKS

This is a society where the group is more significant than the individual. Egyptians love to socialize with their friends, and unmarried Egyptians are unlikely to live on their own.

Social obligations are at the heart of social interaction. If someone is ill, family and friends will readily support them. Likewise, when someone returns from a trip, family and friends will welcome them back with enthusiasm. Friends and relatives call on newlywed couples in their marital abode to congratulate them, and a new mother will be visited with gifts for the baby soon after the birth.

Nobody need ever feel isolated or unsupported. When a husband goes away on a business trip, his wife may be encouraged to stay with her mother for the duration, or a widowed parent may move in with their children. This traditional support network is particularly valuable in a world where social isolation, compounded by busy lifestyles and the convenience of keeping in touch on social media, is intensifying. Strong social networks, family, neighbors, and friends protect their loved ones from isolation. Friends and family gather both on special occasions and in times of crisis.

The family is the most important social unit in Egypt. Family ties are very strong and Egyptian families prioritize and extend moral and, where possible, financial support. Egyptians will commonly ask solo foreigners where their families are, less through nosiness and more because they value the support of families.

Egyptians have many acquaintances and wide social networks and keep friendships alive by visiting often and asking after friends regularly. Neighbors are immediate candidates for friendship. In the older buildings, where families have passed apartments on through the generations, neighbors are close and are a point of call in an emergency. Neighbors in the poorer areas are on especially intimate terms as they need to pool their resources far more often. It is wise for foreigners to be on at least greeting terms with their neighbors, and to observe the Egyptian conventions of modesty and respect when living in a communal building. Advising neighbors and the doorman that you'll be having more than the average number of guests for a party, and there might be louder-than-usual music, would both show respect and be less likely to invite curiosity or grumbles.

Social networks are used in business and in day-to-day

affairs. The personal dimension plays a part in every aspect of life. Personal recommendations are more impressive and have more credibility than a good résumé. It is all about contacts. For example, an Egyptian is unlikely to use a directory to find a plumber but would rather use the services of someone who has been recommended by someone they trust. And a plumber, on his part, will make you a priority if you were mentioned by a client of his.

RELIGION

Islam is the official religion of Egypt, and approximately 90 percent of the population is Sunni Muslim. Apart from tiny Shi'i Muslim and Baha'i communities, the rest of the population is Christian, most belonging to the Coptic Orthodox Church.

Coptic Christianity

One of the world's oldest Christian communities, the Copts are descended from those ancient Egyptians who embraced Christianity in the first century. Coptic, a member of the Hamito-Semitic language group, is the ritual language of the Coptic Church. It is written in the Greek alphabet with some additional letters. The Coptic Church is headed by the pope of Alexandria.

To the foreign eye, Egyptian Copts are indistinguishable from Egyptian Muslims. They share the same value systems and mix in the same circles. Egyptian Copts guard their religion closely, as minorities are inclined to do in any society. Every area has a large church that families attend.

Each family chooses a priest for confession, and he also fulfills the role of family counselor.

Islam

Islam defines not only one's relationship with God, but also all interpersonal relations and daily life. In Egypt Islam is visible, audible, and tangible. The call to prayer resounds from every mosque five times a day, and verses of the Qur'an may be framed and hung on the walls of houses.

Fate plays an important role in popular Islam. This concept underlines the belief that everything that happens in one's life is Allah's will. Among Egypt's largely uneducated lower classes, Islam is intertwined with various practices that are considered contrary to accepted orthodox belief, such as the revering of saints, using magic, and conducting pagan rituals.

Muslims are expected to carry out five duties during their lifetime: the declaration of faith; prayer; charity; fasting; and pilgrimage (if they can). Muslims consider their holy book, the Qur'an, to be the word of God, as dictated to the Prophet Mohammed by the angel Gabriel starting in the month of Ramadan and continuing until the Prophet's death twenty-three years later. The Qur'an is made up of 114 chapters, each called a *sura*, which are divided into verses called *aya*. It addresses questions of behavior, society, and law. After Mohammed received the Qur'an, there was a huge effort to preserve it faithfully, so priority was given to learning the text by heart. It is the primary theological source of Islam. The interpretation of the Qur'an, in theory at least, is constantly evolving and is studied by Islamic theologians to this day.

The second source of Islam, the *hadith*, is the collection of the Prophet's sayings and actions, used to complement the Qur'an as a source of religious and legal guidance for the faithful. The *hadith* was eventually codified.

Although Muslims agree on the basic rules of Islam, various social groups apply religion differently in their daily lives. The rural and lower-middle classes tend to be more observant. The affluent, many of whom have adopted Western ways, consider themselves believers, often guiltily regarding their lifestyle (if it involves drinking and dating freely) as wrong. Egyptians frown upon people who are openly agnostic or atheist. It is, in fact, considered highly offensive for someone to say they do not believe in God.

While Islam is a religion based on clear rules for a life that pleases God, and most Egyptians are conservative Muslims, as with any religion, it is multifaceted in the ways its followers tend to observe it. In recent years Wahhabism, Salafism, and Sufism have grown in popularity.

Wahhabism and Salafism

Wahhabism is a form of Salafism. The terms Salafi and Wahhabi are often used interchangeably, but they are not the same thing. Wahhabism arose in the mid-eighteenth century, while Salafism has existed for hundreds of years and has spread throughout the world. Both groups approach Islamic theology and law literally and conservatively. Egyptian Wahhabism emphasizes consensus in religion rather than pure traditionalism.

Salafis, on the other hand follow the stronger opinion among the Salaf (the "predecessors," or companions of the Prophet Mohammed) based on the Qur'an and the *Sunnah* (the Prophet's traditions). In attempting to maintain Islam's purity, Salafis and Wahhabis reject beliefs and practices not specified by the Qur'an and the Prophet, and deem the glorification of tombs and saints, and the offering of prayers at tombs, to be deviant and heretical.

Sufism is the mystical aspect of Islamic belief and practice, through which believers seek to draw closer to God and to embrace the divine presence in this life by working to restore within themselves the intrinsic, pure, primordial state of *fitra*. There are various Sufi paths designed to bring about direct experience of divine love and wisdom in the world.

Mosques

Cairo is sometimes referred to as "the city of a thousand minarets." Mosques date back to the earliest times in Islam, and were then constructed throughout the Abbasid, Fatimid, Mamluk, and Ottoman periods until the modern day, within a matching range of architectural styles. If you wish to visit a mosque in Egypt, there are certain guidelines and rules to be observed. Note that non-Muslims are not allowed in at prayer time.

- Wear modest clothing. Nobody should wear shorts above the knee. Women should cover their hair (some mosques provide scarves at the entrance), and should be covered except for face, hands, and feet. Loose trousers or long skirts are appropriate, and long, loose shirts. Avoid anything that outlines the contours of the body.
- There are separate entrances for men and women.

Leave your shoes at the entrance.
- You sit on the floor in a mosque, but chairs can be provided for the elderly, the disabled, and pregnant women. Don't lie stretched out on the floor.
- All the general rules of public decorum apply, only more strictly. It is important not to step in front of anyone who is praying.

ATTITUDES TOWARD WOMEN

Egypt is an Islamic society and attitudes to women may not be considered progressive by Western standards. However, the common Western notion that Muslim men consider themselves superior to women is a myth that deserves to be rejected. Islam obliges men to be the protectors and maintainers of women, and to support them financially, and this is the norm rather than the exception in Egypt. As in any society, attitudes toward women range from conservative to liberal. However, it is the case that women are the primary homemakers, and even educated women are not averse to assuming this role. A husband may ask his wife to give up her job in favor of being a wife and mother, and while the educated, professional woman may have a choice, it is unlikely that the rural woman does, or that she would defy her husband's decision.

In recent decades there have been radical changes in the situation of women in education and employment. The number of women in the labor force has grown continuously since the 1960s, and there have been major reforms to the legal status of women. Despite this, gender inequality still exists in Egyptian society.

The gender gap is most evident in the rural areas. Economic pressures on poorer families force many parents to withdraw their children from school to help earn the family's income. Generally, it is the daughters who are pulled out of schools first. These women are likely to marry early and assume a domestic role.

In Egypt, the law does not discriminate between men and women regarding pay. But society puts pressure on women to take on less demanding jobs as their primary duty is in the home. Despite this, many upper- and middle-class women are professionals who juggle work and family. In this context, their status is measured by their husband's wealth and how much domestic help they receive.

A family's honor depends very much on the reputation of its women, which, if tarnished, can damage its social standing. A woman is expected to be a virgin on her wedding day; premarital sex is an absolute taboo (though it may take place discreetly). For this reason, families tend to be stricter with girls than with boys. While Muslim men may marry a Jewish or Christian woman, Muslim women are legally prohibited from marrying out of the faith. Many romances blossom between foreign visitors and Egyptians, and typically a Western man who falls in love with an Egyptian woman and wishes to marry her must either be Muslim or convert. Egyptian Muslim men do not require their Christian or Jewish partners to convert.

A woman's personal status is derived from Islamic law, or *shari'a*, which outlines the rules for marriage, divorce, and inheritance. According to Islamic law, polygamy is allowed: a man may take up to four wives, although this is dependent on his financial ability to provide equally for them. Since 2000, the Egyptian parliament has revised and re-revised the Personal Status Law to provide more equitable rights for women. In Islam, a man could obtain a divorce without his wife's consent. For a woman to obtain a divorce, the burden of proof falls on her to give evidence of wrongdoing. This usually involves a lengthy court procedure, which deters many women from initiating proceedings. The most recent amendment allows women to obtain a divorce quite easily on condition that the husband is exempt from any financial obligations, and, of course, for a woman this is a major consideration—especially if she has been the homemaker and has no skills to offer in the formal working sector. While the laws may have changed to allow a woman to divorce, the social and financial pressures to stay married are obvious, and not unlike those faced by women elsewhere.

The rise of Islamist movements has also reinforced traditional gender roles. Women are seen as the custodians of cultural values and traditions, who take pride in imparting them to the next generation. The adoption of the *hijab*, or head scarf, is the most visible sign of the influence of regional conventions, where, in more conservative Muslim countries, the expression of Islam has become aligned with the outward show of religious observance. Up until the 1990s, Muslim Egyptian women were far freer in their dress choices. Today most Muslim Egyptian women wear the *hijab*. There has also been a noticeable rise in the wearing of the *niqab*, the full-face veil, in recent years, but to assume that these fully veiled women are all Egyptian would be misguided. Egypt, still a centrally located country, has many residents from all over the Middle East.

"*INSHA'ALLAH*"

Egyptians are generally fatalistic and superstitious. Good fortune is God's mercy, and misfortune is His will— whatever happens, good or bad, is considered a blessing. The submission to God is even evident in daily speech. The expression "*insha'Allah*" means "God willing." Egyptians inject this expression into every sentence that denotes intention; not to use it is seen as tempting fate.

Therefore, if talking in the future tense, the word *insha'Allah* must be used. An Egyptian will never say, "I'm going to Alexandria tomorrow." He will most definitely say, "I'm going to Alexandria tomorrow, *insha'Allah*." The final decision is that of God. If one forgets to say *insha'Allah*, someone else will interject with a reminder. For example, if someone asks, "Are you going to Alexandria tomorrow," and the reply is "Yes," the person who asked will often add the missing "*insha'Allah*."

Today, in practice, the use of the word has increased tremendously. It has become the easiest and most noncommittal answer to a question, and might mean, "yes," "probably," "probably not," and "no." It sometimes reaches absurd proportions whereby you ask someone, "Have you finished this task?" and they reply "*insha'Allah*," even if they have finished it! The use of *insha'Allah* may confuse and frustrate many foreigners, but to make a joke about it between foreigner friends in the company of Egyptians would be insulting. In fact, making overt jokes about any religious saying or convention, and most especially Allah, would be unwise.

BACKHAND ECONOMY

Rigid bureaucracy, a freely available but often poorly run educational system, and low wages have allowed corruption to flourish and the sense of social responsibility to diminish somewhat. Many Egyptians bend the rules without compunction because they feel that the top strata of society are far more corrupt. The poor majority, who have little power within the system, tend to think that since they can't change the status quo, there is no point in making huge personal efforts for little in return.

The average Egyptian regularly faces bureaucratic obstacles caused by badly thought-out or implemented procedures, or procedures that are artificially created, so that sometimes the only way forward is by oiling the wheels. However, bribes should never be offered.

WASTA

The support system that Egyptians rely on is provided by their social network, including family, friends, and acquaintances. This has become even more important, especially within the context of an increasingly unpredictable and corrupt state system. Calling old friends for favors and pulling strings is not only the norm, but often the only way of getting what you need or want.

Wasta (connections) are key to getting a good job, sometimes even any job. This means you need to nurture and maintain the contacts you have. Family is usually the first point of call, but they might not have all the necessary connections, so people use friends or acquaintances, depending on their needs. The other side of the coin is that, using *wasta*, people can end up with jobs they are unqualified for or have no interest in. It is often not about what you know but who you know.

The underprivileged class in Egypt, those unlikely to have a strong *wasta*, will often approach figures of authority with an attitude of caution and perhaps even sycophancy.

TOLERANCE AND PREJUDICE

Though conservative in their own society, Egyptians are quite tolerant of Westerners' "strange" customs and generally expect foreigners to be different. There are, however, things that are simply not tolerated.

Homosexuality, while not illegal, is not accepted by Muslims or Christians on either religious or social grounds. However, because it is considered debauchery, homosexuals can be charged under Law 10/1961of the Penal Code, or articles relating to family values in the cybercrime Law 175/2008. There is a homosexual community in Egypt, but they usually guard their private lives carefully and only reveal their sexuality to close, liberal-minded friends who will neither ostracize nor out them. While it is a cultural norm for two men to be seen hugging each other or walking arm-in-arm, displays of romantic, sexual affection between men are not tolerated, and are likely to result in hostility and possibly violence, if not arrest.

Similarly, displays of affection between heterosexual couples are not acceptable. Kissing on the street will attract a great deal of attention and offend those nearby.

Unfortunately, as in most developing societies, the world's population is usually categorized according to a cultural–racial hierarchy, even though Egyptians will most certainly reject any suggestion that they might be racist. Typically, White Westerners are at the top, Egyptians next, then Arabs, followed by Asians, and lastly Africans. While these attitudes are undoubtedly racist, they do not find violent expression toward the local Sudanese, for instance. Racism, where it is found, is at most confined to derogatory comments and/or ridicule.

SENSE OF HUMOR

Centuries of occupation and economic hardship have given the Egyptians a vital means of self-preservation: a sense of humor. Egyptians make fun of social relations, local politics, foreigners, and themselves. Even religion is the subject of jest, within limits, though preferably best left to the Egyptians themselves. In any culture, jokes form around stereotypes, and you may hear Lower Egyptians joking about "a man from the south" (Upper Egyptian), being supposedly tough, stubborn, and stupid.

CHAPTER THREE

CUSTOMS &
TRADITIONS

In Egypt custom and tradition play a central role in people's lives. Though most customs have a religious origin, it is their social function that glues society together.

CALENDARS

In Egypt both the Christian (Gregorian and Coptic) and the Islamic calendars are used. Business generally uses the Gregorian, while religious holidays are dictated by the religious calendars.

The Islamic calendar is based on the phases of the moon and consists of twelve lunar months. The lunar year is 354 days long, so the dates move in relation to the Gregorian calendar. The calendar begins with the Prophet Mohammed's migration from Mecca to Medina in the year 622 CE of the Gregorian calendar.

The Coptic calendar has thirteen months: twelve have thirty days each and the last month has five or six days, depending on whether it is a leap year. This calendar is used today not just by Copts in a religious context, but by all Egyptians. Weather, and agricultural seasons and harvests are referred to using the Coptic calendar. All Egyptians calculate the period of the *Khamsin* (the annual southerly winds and sandstorms) by it.

NATIONAL HOLIDAYS

Public or national holidays are celebrated by the whole country. Some are religious, others are secular; some are fixed, others movable. There are four Islamic and two Christian holidays. Ramadan, although not a national holiday, is the most important month in this predominantly Muslim country.

RAMADAN (MOVABLE)

Ramadan, the ninth month of the lunar Islamic calendar, is when the Qur'an was said to have been revealed to the Prophet Mohammed. During this month all adult Muslims, except for the sick, elderly, and pregnant, fast—abstaining from food, drink, and sex—from sunrise to sunset.

Ramadan is a huge event in Egypt, and a festive spirit sweeps the country. Decorations adorn the streets, households prepare for the event in advance, and business and school hours are altered to accommodate the fasters. It is a wonderful time of year to visit, and foreigners passing by during *iftar* (the breaking of the fast) may be invited to join the locals. As the fast often ends when commuters

Prayers in El-Refa'i Mosque in Old Cairo.

are making their way home, one may see people handing
out water or dates to them during *iftar*, and this kindness
is received with gratitude, particularly if Ramadan falls
during the hot summer months.

Traditionally, people had to wait for the official sighting
of the crescent moon before the fast was declared. Today,
the start date of a lunar month is, of course, known in
advance, but the tradition of spotting the moon has been
upheld. In the old days there would be a procession to a
site where the moon could be seen clearly, and *fawanis*
(lanterns, singular *fanous*) were used to light the way.
Today the *fawanis* have evolved into elaborate decorations
hung outside homes, in the streets, and in shops, and
children are customarily given a colorful lantern.

During Ramadan, the *taraweeh* prayer is performed
every evening in the mosque after the fifth fixed prayer.
While participation is voluntary, this potent prayer is
highly recommended and may also be performed at home.

On the first day of Ramadan, people usually break the fast with their families. The *iftar* is a ceremonious affair that takes a lot of preparation. People wait for the sunset call to prayer before they begin to eat. It was said that the Prophet used to break his fast with a few dates and a glass of milk. Today many people like to keep up this tradition. The *iftar* usually consists of soup and several dishes of meat, rice or pasta, and vegetables.

After the *iftar*, families take their tea and dessert around the television as they watch the array of programs made especially for Ramadan. The huge, guaranteed audience means that most television production companies devote significant budgets to soap operas screened during Ramadan. Actors' celebrity is measured by their appearances at this time. Advertising companies reserve large amounts of money, creativity, and talent for Ramadan advertising.

Iftar during Ramadan in the Khan Khalili Market in Cairo.

Charity and goodwill are important principles in Ramadan. For this reason, it is common for people who have not made it home by *iftar* to be handed a date or fruit by a stranger. Outside mosques, long wooden or plastic tables are laid out with a simple *iftar*, free of charge, for those who are fasting and have nowhere to eat. Even away from mosques, one can see these tables, known as *mawa'id el rahman* (tables of the Merciful), all around the country, set up by wealthy people for those in need. Beggars and street sweepers often line up to get a place at one throughout the month. Even a person who can afford his own *iftar* but has not made it home on time will be welcome: the idea is that no one should be alone during *iftar*. It is common for Egyptians settling down to *mawa'id el rahman* to invite a passerby or a café customer to partake in a meal, and it would be a friendly and respectful gesture to accept graciously and join them.

The *suhur* is the last meal of the day during Ramadan and usually takes place shortly before sunrise, when the next day's fasting begins. It usually consists of *ful* (Egyptian beans), cheese, eggs, yogurt, or any light meal.

In the big cities, the *suhur* has evolved from a necessary meal to a large-scale commercial affair. Today, hotels, companies, and individuals set up Ramadan tents, big marquees that offer a set menu, music, and some form of live entertainment. These range in price and opulence. Some of the larger ones provide a full program in lavish surroundings and sometimes a *wasta* is needed to get in.

At around 3:00 a.m., the *misaharati* (drummer) wanders through the streets of a residential area, beating his drum three times and calling on the faithful to wake up and take their *suhur* before morning prayers: "*Es ha ya nayem Wahed el dayem. Ramadan Karim Es ha ya nayem Wahed el razaq,*" meaning "Awake, oh sleeper and praise Allah. Welcome to you Ramadan, month of forgiveness." Traditionally the *misaharati* knew the people in their neighborhood and would call some of them by their names. As he goes from street to street, his tiny drum makes an astonishingly loud sound that can be heard for several blocks in all directions.

Today people will typically set their alarm clocks to ensure they don't miss the last meal before sunrise. In more affluent areas the *misaharati* has disappeared altogether, while other areas still expect and enjoy the cultural experience of the *misaharati*. The *misaharati's* job is voluntary, but at the end of Ramadan residents will often tip him with food or cash.

With all the spirituality and festivity that sweeps the country at Ramadan, there is also an air of tension in the first few days when people are still adjusting to not eating and drinking. The fasting itself can be difficult, particularly when Ramadan falls in summer: the weather is hot and the days are long. Tempers often flare as people, especially coffee drinkers and smokers, suffer from their respective withdrawal symptoms.

Traffic in the main cities becomes a series of gridlocks as everyone rushes home from work to join friends and family for the *iftar*. Most businesses will devote one day of the month to a company *iftar* at a restaurant.

Foreigners, while not expected to fast, should respect the spirit of Ramadan. It is rude to eat or drink in the street while others are fasting, and it is not unusual for smokers or someone enjoying a beverage in a park to be berated by someone fasting. Most cafés and restaurants are open during Ramadan, so eating and drinking can be done discreetly indoors. Typically, these eateries will draw down their blinds just before *iftar* and staff will take their meal together, and then resume business.

Because it is a sacred month, you will find that most Egyptians dress more modestly during Ramadan. For the same reason, people who drink alcohol during the year typically abstain during this month.

OTHER RELIGIOUS HOLIDAYS

Islamic New Year (Muharram 1)
The start of the Islamic year is the first day of Muharram, the first month of the Islamic lunar calendar. It is a national holiday, and government and religious officials usually mark it with a special function.

Moulid El Nabi (Prophet Mohammed's Birthday) (Rabi al-Awwal 12)
The national holiday celebrating the Prophet's birthday falls in the third month of the Islamic calendar. It is mainly a family occasion, and children dress in their finest clothes and enjoy special sweets, such as *malban* made with additional nuts and dried fruits; girls receive *aruset el mulid*, a small sugar doll, and boys a sugar *houssaan* (horse).

Eid el Fitr (Shawwal 1–3)
Eid el Fitr (*eid* means feast, and *fitr* breaking of the fast) is

a three-day feast that marks the end of Ramadan. On the first day men traditionally head to their local mosque for the communal Eid prayer at sunrise. People greet each other by saying "*Eid Mubarak*" (Blessed Eid). A very important aspect of Eid is charity, and all Muslims who are able are expected to give to the needy.

Eid festivities take place more in the home than on the street. As it is a family celebration, after the Eid prayer it is customary for families to gather for a large lunch, usually at the home of one of the older members. Children are given money and new clothes. Delicious melt-in-your-mouth *kahk* (sweet shortbread biscuits) are offered to guests, and homemakers pride themselves on their special recipes.

Assorted sweets and pastries for Ramadan.

Fatta with white rice, crispy bread, and cow's trotters.

Eid el Adha (Dhu al-Hijjah 10–13)

Falling in the twelfth month of the Islamic calendar, Eid el Adha (feast of the sacrifice) is perhaps the most sacred of the Muslim festivals, as it is a celebration that marks the pilgrimage to Mecca. The four-day feast commemorates the testing of Abraham, who was asked by God to sacrifice his son—Ismail in the Qu'ran, and Isaac in the Bible. Muslims offer a sacrifice of their own by slaughtering an animal and donating most of the meat to the poor.

Egyptians go to the mosque for Eid prayers early in the morning, reciting *takbeer* (proclaiming Allah's greatness) en route. After prayer, families gather at home for a hearty breakfast of *fatta*, a dish made of meat, bread, and rice, topped with vinegar and garlic, and other favorites such as kebab and *kibda* (liver).

Coptic Christmas (January 7)

Coptic Christmas is celebrated on January 7. In 2002, this Coptic festival was declared an official national holiday as a sign of Christian–Muslim unity. Christmas scenes in Egypt are a familiar sight to Westerners with their festive lights and Christmas-themed décor. Christians attend mass on the evening of January 6, and return home to a roast turkey in addition to traditional Egyptian dishes. Families and close friends visit each other and exchange gifts and enjoy the day having tea, *kahk*, and other treats.

Coptic Easter (movable)

Coptic Easter is the most important date of the Egyptian Christian calendar. It sometimes coincides with Easter in the West but could fall up to five weeks later. On this occasion, Copts end a fifty-five-day period of fasting, during which they abstain from animal products. They attend evening mass and return home to a late meal in which meat features prominently. Copts make the same *kahk* for Easter as Muslims do for Eid el Fitr.

Shamm el Nessim (movable)

This feast marking the arrival of spring has been celebrated by Egyptians for 4,500 years. In Ancient Egypt the harvest season was known as *Shamo*. In Arabic, *shamm* means to smell and *nessim* means breeze, so in Arabic the feast is known as the "smelling of the breeze."

The Ancient Egyptians celebrated the beginning of spring by offering *fiseekh* (salted fish), lettuce, and eggs to the gods. The lettuce was said to represent the start of spring, the eggs renewal of life, and the fish fertility. *Fiseekh* is a particularly odorous fish and can be smelled when wandering through the fish markets during the celebration period.

Today the holiday is still celebrated by most Egyptians of all faiths, who eat the same combination of foods. The eggs are dyed and decorated with colorful designs, much like Easter eggs in many Christian countries.

Shamm el Nessim falls on the Monday following the Coptic Easter. As it falls in the mild spring before the summer heat sets in, it is celebrated outdoors. Millions of Egyptians take to the parks and even to small grass patches on islands between highways to "smell the breeze."

SECULAR HOLIDAYS

Apart from the major religious holidays, holidays that fall during the week are not celebrated on the actual date, but on the Thursday of the same week.

Revolution Day and National Police Day (January 25)

January 25 commemorates both the role of the Egyptian police in the toppling of King Farouk in 1952, and the day that marks the end of Mubarak's thirty-year rule (2011). This is the first of two Revolution Days in the Egyptian calendar.

Sinai Liberation Day (April 25)

Sinai Liberation Day commemorates the regaining of the Sinai Peninsula, and the end of the Israeli occupation, on April 25, 1982; it also celebrates April 25, 1988, when the last Israeli soldier left the town of Taba on the Red Sea. This date honors Sinai's significance to Egypt.

Labor Day (May 1)

Labor Day honors the workers, as it does in most other countries in the world. Most public bodies and schools and private businesses are closed on Labor Day.

Liberation Day (June 18)

This commemorates the departure of the last British troops from Egypt in 1956, ending an occupation that had lasted seventy-four years. There are celebrations in schools and universities.

Revolution Day (July 23)

July 23, 1952, marks the day Egypt ceased to be a monarchy and became a republic. Celebrations usually start on July 22, the day the military coup d'état started. On July 23, the president is likely to make a speech and military parades and concerts are held.

Armed Forces Day (October 6)

This day celebrates the Egyptian army's crossing into Sinai in 1973 and its victory over the Israeli forces. Numerous military parties and firework displays are held to honor those lost in the war.

Suez Victory Day (October 24)

This marks the day in 1973 when the port of Suez resisted Israeli air and ground attacks. Residents burned Israeli tanks at the entrance to the city.

Victory Day (December 23)

This celebration takes place mainly in Port Said, and commemorates Egypt's victory over the British, French, and Israelis in 1956.

OTHER CELEBRATIONS

Christmas Day (December 25) and New Year's Day (January 1)

While these are not traditional Egyptian celebrations, today they are popular among the affluent classes. Western (as distinct from Coptic) Christmas is becoming more noticeable in the large cities. It used to be celebrated mainly by the small Catholic community, but it is now fashionable for Westernized Egyptians to have a Christmas tree. Street vendors sell Christmas hats at traffic lights and streets, and businesses and cafés are decorated, especially in areas with foreign residents.

New Year's Eve sees all the five-star hotels booked up with fancy parties, offering buffets, drinks, entertainment, hats, and poppers—in traditional Western festive style.

Mother's Day (March 21)
While not a public holiday, Mother's Day is celebrated by Egyptians of all faiths and classes. Children give their mothers gifts or cards, and television stations broadcast special programs.

MAWALEED

A *mulid* (literally "birthday," plural *mawaleed*) is the celebration of a saint, a custom observed by both Muslims and Christians. *Mawaleed* are sacred events for members of the Sufi order, the mystical branch of Islam. Sanctification of a person is forbidden according to a strict interpretation of Islam, and some consider these celebrations to be *shirk* (sacrilegious). But the tradition continues in parts of the country, especially in rural areas and among the poor. The celebrations fall on specific dates in the Hijri calendar, so they are movable throughout the Gregorian calendar.

Mawaleed are vibrant events, bursting with color and festivity. Most villages and every large city area have their

Whirling dervishes of the Al Tannoura Folklore Troupe at a *mulid* in Cairo.

own saint whose festival is celebrated once a year. The festivities include swings for children, drinking areas for the adults, and booths selling toys. There is singing and dancing, and entertainment, often in brightly colored tents with illuminations. A professional group of people called the *mawaldiya* generally organize *mawaleed* and other occasions. They set it up, dismantle it when it's over, and head off to the next saint's location.

The Sufi sheikhs dress in colorful robes, while whirling dervishes perform their spellbinding routine. Others perform the *zikr*, chanting religious songs to hypnotic rhythms that lead to a state of trance. The atmosphere is alive with incense, music, and prayer.

SUPERSTITION

People from all segments of Egyptian society are generally superstitious. Egyptians believe that if someone is envious of you, they can cast the evil eye on you and cause your good luck to disappear. For this reason they practice discretion. For fear of attracting the evil eye they are unlikely to reveal a new job until the start date, or to talk about a salary raise.

There are certain ways to ward off the evil eye, such as reading certain verses of the Qur'an, burning incense, or using a protective blue bead.

A new car is likely to have a copy of the Qur'an placed in it somewhere.

A new house is blessed with a mixture of frankincense and *bukhoor* (Arabic gum), while a new baby may wear a little brooch with a blue bead on it.

When paying a compliment, one must add the words *Masha' Allah* to show that your intentions are good and that you are not trying to cast the evil eye on someone or something. Thus, if admiring a new home, you should say "*Masha' Allah*, what a lovely house."

If a person comes into some good fortune, they should share it with others, otherwise superstition has it that their luck will run out. If someone buys a new home, for example, they should slaughter an animal as a sacrifice and share the meat with the poor.

Owls and black cats are considered bad omens and bearers of bad news. Egyptians won't leave shoes upside down because it is said that the sole of the shoe should not face God. Open scissors are a sign of bad luck.

The holy book of Islam, the Qur'an, should be treated with respect. Nothing should be placed on top of it and it should not be placed on the floor.

CHAPTER FOUR

MAKING FRIENDS

Egyptians are friendly and hospitable, and it is easy to strike up a conversation with them and for a friendship to develop. Meet one Egyptian and you are likely to be introduced to their extended social network, but deeper friendships are acquired through repeated interaction over time. Egyptians put a lot of time and effort into developing friendships, expecting trust and commitment in return. Any disagreements that arise between friends are forgiven simply because the two parties have known each other for so long. Egyptians will often refer to *el 'ishra* (the long time spent together).

The Westernized upper classes, a tiny minority, socialize in a similar fashion to the West. Men and women mix freely, and dating is not uncommon; they go to parties, mingle at bars, and take weekend trips to the desert or beach resorts. Most of the population, however, especially in rural areas, is more conservative, and socializing will probably take place in a family setting. Families visit each other frequently and their children get to know each other from an early age. In the cities, friendships develop at

Friends posing for a street photographer on the waterfront in Alexandria.

school or at university and people will often socialize with the same group for years. Male–female friendships are not permitted in conservative communities but are common among city dwellers. However, once they have married, male–female friendships are unlikely to occur.

Though the rules for Egyptian–Egyptian friendships may be rigid—people instinctively mix with their own social class and tight networks can be difficult to break into—they are more relaxed for foreigners. Egyptians are very open to foreigners, and usually double their efforts to ensure that their foreign friends feel welcome.

Egyptians are hospitable and generous and will happily invite friends for meals, buy them gifts, and offer their time. They do this from the perspective that real friendships are long-term, and gestures of kindness and hospitality are reciprocated, even if not immediately.

Society imposes stricter rules on girls than on boys. In the rural and poorer classes, it is common for boys to socialize outside the house in groups, but the girls are often housebound. When girls are allowed to go out, they are usually subject to strict parent-imposed curfews.

ATTITUDES TOWARD FOREIGNERS

Most foreigners visiting Egypt are tourists, and the Egyptians are used to the idea of them coming and going without making any long-term friendships locally. But increasingly, digital nomads are settling in the coastal towns and there are growing numbers of foreign teachers at the many international schools. Nevertheless, Egyptians are gracious and hospitable, and any foreigner who shows respect for Egyptian culture is warmly embraced.

Wealthy, urban Egyptians are the most likely to be well traveled or educated abroad. They relate to foreigners easily and make friends with them. The less educated Egyptians often have misguided perceptions of foreigners. Their main window into the lifestyle and behavior of foreigners is via the mass media, particularly television and more specifically soap operas and music videos. To them, life abroad resembles Universal Studios and is deeply coveted by many youngsters, frustrated with their lives and dwindling opportunities in Egypt.

Because foreign television series and soap operas shape their perceptions of Western women and their relations with men, Egyptian men may interpret a foreign woman's short skirt or revealing blouse or her ease of conversation with a man as a sign of sexual availability.

In Egypt, the common word for a foreigner is *agnabi* for a man and *agnabiya* for a woman (*aganeb* is the plural). While many traditional Egyptians see foreigners as materially and perhaps intellectually advanced, they also regard them as morally inferior. As Egyptians are community orientated—children stay at home until they are married and the elderly are taken care of by their families—they are often appalled by the fact that in the West children leave the family home prior to marriage, and the elderly are sent to nursing homes. This seeming lack of social cohesion or community care represents a lack of family values to Egyptians. This does not mean that Egyptians are not open to relationships with *aganeb*. But for harmonious relationships, respect for the culture is paramount. Egyptians will cherish a foreigner who does not flaunt his or her own ways or try to "educate" them, but rather appreciates Egyptian attitudes and customs.

GREETINGS

Greetings are very important, and many Egyptians form their opinion of someone based on how they greet them. Warmth is fundamental, even in formal settings. Egyptians make a distinction between formality and coldness. You can be formal but warm; for example, a firm handshake can be accompanied by a smile.

People of the same sex greet each other with affection. It is common for women to kiss on both cheeks when they meet, while in rural areas they kiss more than once on each cheek and may kiss the hand of an elderly relative to show respect. Men who know each other well also kiss each other on both cheeks. A pat on the back is an extra sign of

Chance meeting in the park.

warmth. Handshakes between men should be strong and firm, as limp handshakes are considered insincere. It is also common to see men walking together holding hands or arm-in-arm, and foreigners should guard against assuming this to be an indication of sexual orientation. It is not.

The rules are different for relations with the opposite sex, where minimal physical contact is the norm. A polite brief handshake is acceptable. A man should not extend his hand to a woman he does not know well; he should wait for her to extend her hand first. Public displays of affection are unacceptable, even between husband and wife.

It is rude to see an acquaintance and not greet them, even if they seem busy or are engaged in conversation with someone else. A distant wave is considered rude.

Verbal greetings can be rich and flowery and vary according to the situation. The most straightforward greeting when meeting someone or arriving at a place is *salamu 'aleikom,* which literally means "peace be upon you." The reply to that would be *wa 'aleikom el salam*, "and peace be upon you." It is rude not to reply to that specific greeting, even if it is not personally directed at you.

The standard morning greeting is *sabah el kheir*, which means "morning of goodness." In reply one can repeat *sabah el kheir* or, more warmly, offer *sabah el nur* ("morning of light").

HOSPITALITY

The Egyptians are masters of hospitality. If they think you may be dining alone, they may insist on inviting you home for dinner. They will insist on paying when out for dinner.

If dining out with an Egyptian who insists on paying the bill, the guest should also insist on paying. Most of the time, there will be a push and pull and it is the person with the strongest will who finally pays. If you are paid for, it is polite to return the invitation on a later occasion.

As in many cultures, in Egypt guests are honored, particularly if they are foreign, as Egyptians feel responsible for their well-being. They are genuinely concerned about the visitor's comfort and satisfaction with their trip and go out of their way to show the good side of Egypt.

It is rare to go to an Egyptian's house and not be served something to eat or drink and most probably both. Even if you arrive on short notice, it is highly likely that the host has something in the kitchen "just for guests."

Failure to show is considered extremely rude, and if you can't make an invitation, it is good form to let the host know as soon as possible.

INVITATIONS HOME

When invited to lunch or dinner at an Egyptian's home, it is polite to accept and to bring a dessert. There are numerous pastry shops where you can pick up a plate of Arabic sweets or a cake. Do not bring alcohol, unless you know the person very well and are certain that they drink. Flowers, while appreciated in certain Westernized homes, are considered useless by most Egyptians.

Egyptian women put a lot of effort into providing a big spread for their guests. Lunches or dinners are times when the woman of the house can showcase her culinary skills. Even in modest homes, guests are rarely invited for just a pasta and salad.

The Egyptians might not always be punctual, but this is usually because of traffic congestion, which is unpredictable. If a dinner invitation is set for 8:00 p.m., aim for punctuality and advise the host or hostess if you are running late. It is polite to wait for all the guests to arrive before serving the meal. The women of the house (wife and daughters) will be in the kitchen applying the final touches and will join the guests at the table. It is courteous for female guests to offer to help in the kitchen, even if the offer is rejected.

Meals are not served in courses, but rather all the dishes are placed in the middle of the table. When the meal is over, the hosts will lead the guests to the sitting area to have tea or coffee with the dessert.

In rural areas, it is customary for the hosts not to eat with the guests. A table is prepared for the visitors and the hosts disappear until they have finished eating. This is so that they can eat their fill without feeling shy.

At the end of the evening, hosts will walk their guests to the door; they never shut the front door before the guests are out of sight.

MANNERS

It is polite to wait to be served at a meal. If you finish what's on your plate, you will typically be given another portion: a clear plate means that you are still hungry. Because the women have spent so much time in the kitchen preparing the food, it is polite to compliment their cooking. An appropriate expression is *teslam edeiki*, which means "bless your hands."

It is considered impolite to leave immediately after a meal. Wait until after coffee and dessert have been served before gently offering your good-byes.

Many Egyptian men smoke freely at most outings and at home. In traditional households a young man is unlikely to smoke in front of his father or an elder as a sign of respect. It is uncommon for women to smoke in public.

DATING

Young adults freely socialize in groups and date much like their Western counterparts, though in some conservative families there are restrictions. Couples go on regular dates to movies, cafés, concerts, festivals, and parks. Some use Western dating apps like Tinder, but Badoo is also popular, as are several other regional sites and apps. However,

Couple in Al Azhar Park, Cairo.

visitors wishing to date should avoid Tinder, as in Egypt it is used by people looking for easy sex or for someone to exploit. That's not to say you can't find genuine friendship there or a possible date, but err on the side of caution.

Egyptian dating customs are conservative and traditional compared to the West. Many young Egyptians meet potential partners through family or friends, and strict gender roles and expectations are the norm in conservative areas. Men typically take the lead initiating and planning dates and are expected to pay for the meal and entertainment. Public displays of affection are not acceptable, and couples behave modestly and respectfully in public. In strict families, there may be no dating at all prior to marriage, or it may be limited to chaperoned or group outings. While most Egyptians largely adhere to the dating rules, the younger generations are more open to new ideas and different ways of meeting partners.

CHAPTER FIVE

PRIVATE AND FAMILY LIFE

Most of Egypt's population live near agricultural land. However, about thirty years ago, as overpopulation resulted in a scarcity of land, people began to migrate to the cities. Many still maintain their ties with their original villages and return on special occasions.

In the cities, most housing consists of apartments, either in purpose-built blocks or, more rarely, in old converted villas. Many people who inherit villas sell them to developers, who typically rent them out to companies. Mostly, however, they tear them down and build large apartment blocks to accommodate the growing population. To escape the overcrowding, pollution, and traffic congestion, wealthy Egyptians favor the new housing developments that have mushroomed on the outskirts of the big cities. These gated compounds provide a safe and clean community space, at a price well beyond the reach of ordinary Egyptians.

The interiors of homes vary aesthetically according to class and income. The style in most urban homes is eclectic, bringing together different cultural influences—

Islamic, French, and Ottoman—which Western aesthetes might find a touch over the top. Furniture in this ornate style is readily available as Egyptian carpenters and craftsmen have mastered the art of its elaborate woodwork.

Rural houses are built of brick. Village furnishings tend to be rustic, with cushions or couches lining the walls in the space reserved for guests and family gatherings. Most homes have a television set, which provides the evening entertainment.

THE HOUSEHOLD

The Egyptian household is family based, with the father at the head. It consists of the nuclear family, and possibly the extended family, but is unlikely to include nonrelatives. Children move out of their parents' homes only to move into their new marital homes, and may return in the case of a divorce. Elderly parents move in with their children when they can no longer look after themselves. As we've seen, it would be shameful to place the elderly in a retirement home.

In a traditional Egyptian family roles are clearly defined. The husband is the breadwinner and the boss. However, the wife is a key decision-maker, and is typically in charge of household spending. Even if an Egyptian woman is employed outside the home, she is still expected to take care of domestic duties, which include shopping, cooking, cleaning, and looking after the children. Egyptian women are house-proud and care about their domestic reputation.

The eldest son usually takes over family responsibilities when the father reaches retirement age or is incapable of working. Traditionally, younger members of the family defer to older members, and women to men. But in a rapidly changing society, middle- and upper-class women are increasingly free of these restrictions as they engage in public life, and they may share the decision-making and the daily chores with their husbands.

GROWING UP IN EGYPT

In Egypt, children are considered a blessing. They are loved and pampered first and disciplined when they are a little older. Egyptian mothers are well known to fuss over their children and see no wrong in them, as illustrated in the expression: "*el ird fi 'ain ommo ghazal*," "the monkey is a gazelle in his mother's eye."

Children in Quseir, on the Red Sea coast.

The idea of hiring a babysitter is totally alien, as family members are always available for this support role, and children are welcomed at most places—they often accompany their parents to restaurants, cinemas, and dinner in other people's homes. It is normal for strangers to be affectionate and tactile with children. Don't be surprised if a friendly restaurant worker picks up your child or if a stranger offers them candies or treats.

Life changes for many children once they start school. The school years put enormous pressure on pupils and families. There is a lot of homework, and free time is filled with private lessons to compensate for an inadequate educational system. Educational extras place a strain on incomes, and secondary school students are under great pressure to pass their *thanawiyya 'amma*, the final exam.

Egyptian students' career prospects are determined by their success in their final exams. Faculties are open only to those who make the cut, but even if students make it to university and graduate, they face the reality of slim job prospects, unless they have social connections. Young people may end up working not in their chosen field, if they get work at all. Each year hundreds of thousands of new graduates compete for a finite number of jobs, resulting in many accepting menial work, or jobs for which they're overqualified, or looking for opportunities abroad.

The *Nadi*

On the social front, many middle-class children and young teenagers go to the *nadi* (social club). Set up in the late nineteenth century for expatriate British families, these clubs offered sports and recreational facilities, including tennis courts, swimming pools, horse-riding, tea gardens, and so on. Membership became open to Egyptians only in the 1940s and depended on status. After the Revolution these clubs were nationalized, and membership was opened to all. Today some clubs receive money from the government and are run by the Ministry of Youth and Sports, while those favored by the upper middle class require family lifetime subscriptions that are phenomenally expensive. Children and their families spend much of their spare time in these clubs and develop social networks that can last a lifetime.

Cafés

European-style cafés are found in almost every city block and have a big social impact. They are a favorite hangout for wealthy teenagers and housewives. The teenagers meet there after school or university and on weekends. They spend hours sipping cappuccinos and lattes, taking selfies, and smoking (often behind their parents' backs). In the evenings, girls generally have earlier curfews than boys.

Education

The education system went through a massive overhaul after the 1952 Revolution. Previously fewer than 50 percent of primary-age children attended school. Today at least 80 percent do, and 68 percent attend secondary school.

The Revolution dramatically expanded educational opportunities. Free education became available to all. Government spending on education increased, and with it the number of primary schools. But this rapid increase came at the expense of quality. A growing population put strains on resources, resulting in overcrowded classrooms and school buildings in disrepair. Given the very large student-to-teacher ratio, parents resorted to private lessons to supplement their children's studies. The decline in the standard of public schooling created a space for private providers, and today there are many foreign-language or international schools that typically include a healthy complement of foreign staff, giving parents the reassurance of a "better" education.

Today the Egyptian middle and upper classes choose to send their children to private schools. The best of these foreign-language schools teach in English or French, and Arabic is relegated to a second language (thus children can spend their entire lives in Egypt and yet have poor Arabic). Graduating from these schools helps facilitate entrance to foreign universities, both locally and abroad. Notable schools in Egypt include Victoria College (founded in 1902) in Alexandria, which counts the late King Hussein of Jordan, professor of literature and public intellectual Edward Said, and the financial pioneer Gilbert de Botton among its many esteemed alumni.

School is compulsory for the first nine years. However, this is not always practical or affordable, particularly in rural areas where families may remove their children from school and send them to work at a young age. The government does not enforce attendance strictly.

Apart from the old established Egyptian universities, which teach in Arabic, there has been a boom in private and foreign universities (sometimes affiliated with universities abroad). The most prestigious of these is the American University in Cairo, alma mater of Queen Rania of Jordan.

National Service

Military service is compulsory for males between the ages of eighteen and thirty. They must have male siblings (an only son is exempt) and be physically and mentally fit. Those in full-time education are excused until they finish their studies. The length of service ranges from one year for those with a university education to three years for those without. Before the 1952 Revolution conscription could be avoided if one paid a sum of money to the government, but afterward this option was abolished.

National service is a miserable and demoralizing experience for most conscripts, as in many armies across the world, and they typically must tolerate repeated bullying in the name of discipline. Without completing their national service, men cannot apply for a passport, which reduces their ability to work, travel, or join family abroad.

There are, of course, those who go on to have a career in the army. For young men with an education, the army is one way of guaranteeing a government job that pays relatively well, provides benefits, and grants power and social status. For those with no education, it can be their only chance of a paid job.

FAMILY OCCASIONS

Family occasions are important and colorful affairs, steeped in tradition and ritual. The help and participation of family members is considered an obligation.

Birth

In the cities, women generally give birth in hospitals attended by a doctor. In rural areas, they are more likely to give birth at home assisted by a midwife and in the company of female family members.

About a week after the birth a *subu'* (birth party) is given for the baby, and friends and acquaintances bring gifts. A customary gift is gold jewelry, regardless of the baby's sex. Babies can accumulate a large amount of jewelry this way, which is generally put away for their future. At the party children are given gifts and candies, adults sugared almonds. Songs are sung, women ululate, and the newborn is dressed in a special white gown.

All Egyptian boys, Christian as well as Muslim, are circumcised, usually a few days after birth. Traditionally there was a party for this event, particularly in rural areas, but today this is less common, as boys are generally circumcised in a hospital or clinic.

Lineage is important and is made official by registering the newborn's name. Theoretically an Egyptian's full name is never-ending. A baby is given a name, which is followed by the father's first name, then the grandfather's first name, then the great-grandfather's name, and so on. In official documents and for proof of identity Egyptians use three or four of these names. Socially, the first name and the surname are used. Thus, if a Mohamed Badawi has a son called Ahmed, his name is Ahmed Mohamed Badawi. If Ahmed's wife gives birth to a baby girl and calls her Layla, her name is Layla Ahmed Mohamed Badawi. Socially, people will call her Layla Badawi. Foreigners required to complete official forms can expect to be asked to supply their first name followed by their father's name and should duly state their maiden name or married surname.

Engagement and Marriage

Marriage is the most important rite of passage and celebration in an Egyptian's life. For most men, it marks their transition into adulthood, while for women, it is the beginning of the road to motherhood. In a society where family is important, the young are eager to start their own.

Romantic relationships are difficult to sustain. Unless they are formally engaged, it is rare for unmarried couples to meet without a chaperone and arranged marriages are common. Introduction to a suitable spouse typically comes about through a family member. Bridal consent for the marriage is very important and is required by religion, and rarely will anyone be forced into a marriage. If a couple develops a relationship outside the family setting, family approval of the union is essential. Egyptians regard marriage not only as a union of individuals but a marriage of families. In-laws interact with each other frequently.

Weddings are a time of joy in most families, with much pomp and ceremony surrounding the event. However, there is also a huge financial burden. Parents of the bride and groom contribute differently to the wedding costs.

The process begins when the groom's family makes an appointment with the prospective bride's family to ask for her hand in marriage. The groom reveals his income and states the amount of *muqaddam* (dowry) he is prepared to pay; a groom must pay the dowry before the consummation of the marriage. If the bride's family accepts, they seal the bond by reading a specific verse of the Qur'an called the *fatha*. The parents then set a date for the engagement, which is usually a small party at the bride's house. During the engagement, rings are worn on the right hand and are switched to the left hand on the wedding day.

The engagement period allows the couple freedom to go out unchaperoned. It is also the time to get their new home ready. The groom's family traditionally provides the house and the bride's is responsible for furnishing it. Couples who cannot afford a home may move in with the groom's family.

Henna Night

When a woman is to be married, a celebration is held for her called *leilet el henna* (night of the henna). Her female relatives and friends gather to sing, dance, and perform a set of rituals to bless her approaching marriage. Her hands are dotted with henna paste, a tradition dating back to the time when henna was used cosmetically.

The Wedding

Egyptian wedding parties are grand occasions, and, depending on the family's income, will be celebrated more or less lavishly with food, music, and entertainment. The groom's family traditionally pays for the wedding ceremony. However, as wedding parties have become such extravagant affairs among the well-to-do, the couple's families may choose to split the costs. The *zaffa*, the procession, is an adrenalin-pumped event that announces that a wedding is taking place. While the procession is open to all to enjoy and accompany the bridal couple to their destination, the reception is for invited guests only.

In some rural areas the couple's furniture is paraded through the town on its way to its new home.

Marriage in Egypt is a civil contract and is usually performed by an official. Religious ceremonies are part of the process but cannot replace the civil element. Egyptian women retain their original family name after marriage.

Death

Being religious people, Egyptians consider death to be the will of God. Grief is expressed openly. Islamic tradition dictates that burial takes place within twenty-four hours of death, except in extraordinary circumstances.

On the day of the funeral and after the sunset prayers, people wishing to pay their respects attend a mosque where the family of the deceased has arranged a Qur'an reading. As the sheikh recites the Qur'an verses, the mourners pay their respects to the bereaved. The sheikh will take a break every half hour, and it is advisable to wait for one of these breaks before leaving the gathering. Plain Turkish coffee is served at these occasions. Men are expected to wear formal dress and dark ties, and women to dress in black to show their respect. Women are received either in a separate hall at the same mosque, or at the house of the deceased.

A three-day mourning period follows the burial. Relatives wear black during this time and a wife who has lost her husband is expected to wear black for a year; however, many widows never revert to colored clothing. Family and close friends attend to the needs of the bereaved and may move in for the mourning period.

Seven days after the death, there is a reading of the Qur'an. Family and close friends gather at the house of the

deceased, where each person will read a section.
Forty days after the death, another service takes place
at the house.

In Egypt flowers are not sent at funerals—they are
typically reserved for celebrations. To send flowers to a
funeral would be an immense faux pas, as it would imply
that the funeral is a happy occasion.

DAILY LIFE

In the Town

Internal migration has put huge pressure on Egypt's towns
and cities and resulted in extreme overcrowding. Town
planning is very weak and infrastructure often doesn't
meet the area's needs. For example, there is no drainage
on roads in high rainfall areas such as Alexandria.

The routine of urban life pretty much mirrors that
in the West. People commute to work and socialize on
weekends and holidays. While economic pressures,
overcrowding, traffic congestion, and pollution can make
daily life a grind, social life helps to alleviate the stress.

Egyptians will typically encourage foreigners living in
Egypt to make their own meals from scratch: supermarket
produce is considered expensive and inferior. Egyptian
women are enthusiastic cooks who prefer to start
from the basics, buying fresh fruit and vegetables from
the grocer, meat from the butcher, and fish from the
fishmonger. They are likely to favor a particular shop
and will assure you of the quality of their produce.

Urban Networking

Urban households also have a small network of people outside the family who provide essential services—the *bowab* (doorman), the *baqqal* (grocer), and the *makwagi* (ironing person). The *bowab* is on-site, the grocer and the laundry service usually no more than a block or two away.

The *bowab*'s official job is to act as a security guard, but he can be a caretaker, a runner of errands, and the person who washes your car. He usually lives in a small room in the building and gets a modest stipend from the residents.

In Egypt most *baqqaleen* (the plural of *baqqal*) deliver groceries to your door. Daily needs such as bread, milk, butter, canned goods, and bottled water are just a phone call away. Once a relationship has been developed with the local *baqqal*, one can use a credit system and pay at the end of the month. In more middle- to upper-class areas, residents use centralized delivery services, usually available on a mobile app, and order their groceries or meals from local restaurants in this way.

Most areas have a local *makwagi*. Send your clothes in a bag and they will be returned cleaned, pressed, and folded or on hangers. It's cheaper than a hotel laundry service.

In the Country

Rural life is far more conservative. The family hierarchy is more rigid, with men exercising unquestionable authority. Fewer women work outside the home. The pace of life is rhythmic. Farmers wake at dawn and go to their local mosque to pray. They spend the day working in the fields, breaking for noon prayers. They return home for a meal and a rest and may go back to the fields later. There will be a light evening meal with the family.

Ambitions in the rural areas used to be simple: people wanted a home, a family, and land to cultivate. As the children grew up, they helped on the land, so they were an investment and a form of social security for the parents.

Nasser's Revolution changed the dynamics. Farming was regulated; land was taken from the big estate owners and distributed among the agrarian dwellers, who were given land titles. Deeds were inherited, which meant that land was divided between children and then grandchildren. Population growth has diminished the availability of land and families today barely produce enough to sustain themselves, let alone a surplus.

However, with land scarcity and migration to the towns and cities, rural families are now choosing to secure their children's futures by supporting their education rather than expecting them to work in agriculture. As this involves an additional financial burden, many are deciding to have fewer children.

Fashion

Up until the 1970s, most urban Egyptian women wore European dress, which was a statement of modernity and secularism, in sharp contrast to rural dress, which consisted of a long, loose garment and a head scarf. Old Egyptian movies show most women unveiled, but that has changed dramatically with the influence of the Muslim Brotherhood, Wahhabi pressure, and migrant workers returning from conservative Gulf countries wanting to emulate the modesty practiced there.

Upper-class urban Egyptian women still sport Western clothes, but the Islamist trend means that most Egyptian women today cover their heads. You can see a range of styles, from the *gallabiyya*

Fashion shoot in Cairo.

(traditional long, loose robe) and *hijab* (head scarf), to jeans and fashionable tops with creative head coverings.

While women are theoretically free to choose what they wear, some professional Egyptian women do complain of peer pressure in the workplace to be veiled or to cover their arms fully. Yet other women complain of not being given jobs they are qualified for because they are veiled, and prospective employers make removing the *hijab* a condition of employment.

CHAPTER SIX

TIME OUT

Egyptians, who enjoy their weekend on a Friday, love socializing outdoors, taking walks or boat trips, or having picnics. But the hot weather and financial constraints mean that most activity takes place indoors, generally in people's homes. Those who can afford to eat out usually do so in groups. Tables for six are far more common than tables for two. Watching life go by is a favorite pastime, as families or friends congregate in the outdoor spaces to enjoy drinks and *shisha* (water pipes), or play backgammon.

THE NILE

The Nile is the Egyptian playground, toward which people gravitate for many of their social activities. Party boats zip up and down, blaring out loud Arabic music to the cheers and claps of the passengers. Large cruise boats crawl along, hiding from view the belly dancers and the lavish buffets inside. And if you want to join the well-to-do parading their yachts on the Nile, you can rent your own.

Still available are romantic *felucca* trips; a sunset on this type of traditional sailboat is magical. *Feluccas* can be rented in half-hour slots. They are usually crewed by professionals, and you can bring your own food and music.

The banks of the Nile are the setting for many activities. There are restaurants and bars where the well-heeled go to dine and dance. Brides and grooms have their photographs taken next to the Nile, accompanied by large numbers of relatives. Fishermen set up tables and chairs and linger for hours waiting for a catch. Young couples, who have few places to go to in public, line the banks with their backs toward society's prying eyes.

Astute vendors never miss an opportunity to profit from all the activity, selling everything from balloons for children to corn on the cob and grilled sweet potato. Cold drinks, hot drinks, toys, and fake Rolex watches can all be bought al fresco.

SHOPPING FOR PLEASURE

There is an array of places at which to shop, from upmarket boutiques to open-air bazaars. American-style malls have seen a surge in popularity in recent years. The main cities all have malls with multiplex cinemas, shops, and cafés, and international brand stores. Young people treat malls like their community clubs: they meet there, window-shop, sip fruit juice, and mingle in the comfort of the air-conditioning.

Egyptians prefer to buy their spices, clothes, jewelry, and household goods at the open-air markets, which generally operate from 10:00 a.m. to around 10:00 p.m. All shops close during the Friday prayer.

To avoid disappointment at not being able to buy some trinket that has caught your eye, it's best to take cash to markets and informal shops. You are unlikely to find vendors with card transaction machines, commonly called Visa Machines, in these establishments, and even less likely to find ATMs for cash withdrawals.

It is also better to pay in cash as all shops must pay a commission on credit card sales and will therefore charge you more, even if they offer the facility.

In high tourist areas most shopkeepers will try to lure you into their shops with promises of bargains and discounts. Bargaining is an expected part of the process at bazaars and open-air markets. Experienced shoppers will tell you that there are certain tricks to getting a good bargain. First, don't waste your and the seller's time haggling over something that costs very little. Don't haggle unless you intend to buy. Striking a deal is a verbal contract and it is considered rude to reach agreement on a price and then walk away without buying, especially if you have spent some time bringing the price down.

Beware of guides who insist on taking you to a specific shop for items that are sold in many places. They may be getting a commission, which is sure to push up prices. Some savvy vendors have been known to trap naïve travelers into buying with sensational claims. If someone trying to sell you incense tells you it is the same one that Cleopatra used, it probably isn't . . .

In modern supermarkets and malls haggling is not practiced; the price you see is the price you pay.

BARGAINING TECHNIQUE

There are several techniques to haggling: this is just one. If you see something you like, inquire about something else first. Being too eager sends the price up automatically. Eventually, turn the shopkeeper's attention to the item you originally wanted and ask the price. Say you will check elsewhere and be back. Do the same at several shops. When you have a reasonable idea of what it costs generally, you can then return to one of the shops and begin the real bargaining.

Don't look excited about an item; rather, try to find fault with it. The seller knows this is part of the game. When he feels you are truly interested in buying, he may offer you tea and make conversation. Once you've agreed on a price that you feel comfortable with, shake hands, and pay.

CULTURAL ACTIVITIES

Cinema

Egypt has had a strong cinematic tradition since the 1930s, and movies produced there are watched across the Arab world. The golden age of Egyptian cinema was in the 1940s and '50s. Nasser is rumored not to have gone to bed at night without watching an American Western, and Sadat apparently almost missed the coup because he was watching movies with his family. The movie industry took a dip between the 1970s and the new millennium but seems to have bounced back with both commercial films and documentaries being made.

Cinemas are found in the main cities and malls. Sadly, many of the grand cinemas built during Egyptian cinema's heyday are run down or have closed. All movies are subject

The Art Deco design of Cinema Miami in downtown Cairo.

to Egypt's censor: scenes involving sex, extreme violence, or anything considered blasphemous will be cut out.

Theater

Theater in Egypt can be said to date back thousands of years. There is archaeological evidence of storytelling and performance in Ancient Egypt, but the exact nature of this is unclear. Theater as we know it in Egypt today has its roots in the Islamic era—in the Mamluk and Ottoman periods, when theatrical performances took place during religious festivals and in marketplaces.

The Greeks and Romans had introduced plays as a form of entertainment, but Western-style theater really took off during the French campaign in 1789, and almost a century later Khedive Ismail built the French Comedy Theatre and the Opera House as part of the opening celebrations for the Suez Canal. Early Egyptian productions were heavily influenced by European culture, but they evolved over time to incorporate native forms and themes, and plays were performed in Arabic. Notable Egyptian playwrights from the 1950s include Tawfik Al Hakim, Alfred Farag, Youssef Idris, and Noaman Ashour. Comedy classics of the 1970s such as *Madraseit El Moshaghbeen* (*The School of Troublemakers*, 1973) and *Al Motazawegoon* (*The Married Couples*, 1978) are still appreciated by Egyptians today.

During the 1980s the influx of foreign films affected live audience attendance. However, the 2011 Revolution inspired the production of politically charged plays and many young Egyptians are using theater and the other performing arts to express themselves in poetry, dance, and writing. Today, theater is an important aspect of

Egypt's cultural landscape, with many talented directors, playwrights, and actors creating innovative and thought-provoking productions that reflect both the country's history and contemporary social issues.

Music

Music is as old as civilization itself in Egypt. The cow goddess Bat, considered the inventor of music, was often associated with the sistrum, a percussive instrument. Many ancient tomb wall paintings and unearthed treasures attest to the importance of music. In the Neolithic period (c. 4400 BCE) small shells were used as whistles, while during the Predynastic Egyptian period funerary chants were accompanied by clappers. Strong evidence of harps, flutes, and double clarinets exists from the Old Kingdom, and percussion instruments and lutes are evident in

Musicians and dancers in a fresco from the Tomb of Nebamun, c. 1420–1375 BCE

the orchestras of the Middle Kingdom. Cymbals often accompanied music and dance troupes.

Early Egyptian music was influenced by the Romans and Byzantines who had in turn been influenced by earlier Semitic, Ancient Egyptian, and Greek music. During the Medieval Egyptian period some puritanical religious groups were opposed to music on the grounds that it was sinful or immoral. Particularly influential were the Almohads, a Berber Muslim dynasty that ruled much of North Africa and Spain in the twelfth and thirteenth centuries. Known for their strict interpretation of Islamic law, they strongly disapproved of art and music, believing them to be a distraction from the worship of Allah that would lead to immoral behavior; they also associated music with Christian and Jewish culture.

Despite this censorious view, however, music remained entrenched in Egyptian society. *Alateeyeh* (male singers)

Musicians and singers perform songs from Egypt's folk tradition.

were like professional minstrels, hired to sing on special occasions. Unfortunately, their occupation was not well thought of. *Awalim* (female singers), ironically, were better paid and more highly regarded. Typically, they performed hidden from view, and were often hired by a harem master to entertain important guests. The songs of the period were simple, performed within a small range of tones, and quite similar sounding. Though simple, they were embellished with distinct enunciation and in a quavering voice.

Egyptian music began to be recorded in the 1910s and popular songs, both traditional and contemporary, expressed the daily lives and struggles of ordinary people. Classical Egyptian composers and singers of the twentieth century include Sayed Darwish, Umm Kulthum, and Abdel Halim Hafez. Cairene Fatma Said was the first Egyptian soprano to sing at La Scala, Milan, and was a participant in BBC's Radio 3 New Generation Artists Scheme in 2016–18.

Religious music continues to feature in traditional Sunni Muslim and Coptic celebrations. Contemporary Egyptian folk music is still rooted in traditional musical forms, in terms of the instruments used as well as its percussive features and rhythms. Nubian music is typically accompanied with a drum and hand clapping. Ali Hassan Kuban earned the title of the Godfather of Nubian music by infusing traditional Nubian music with jazz. Sa'idi (Upper Egyptian) music is played with drums, flutes, oboes, and two-stringed fiddles and has a strong folk flavor infused with classic and popular music.

Shaabi , meaning "of the people," is a very popular type of Arabic street music. A famous example is the song "Shik Shak Shok," released in the 1970s. Associated with the teaching of belly dancing, its lyrics make a call to abandon Western music and embrace national music and *baladi* dance. The second version of the song, released in the 1990s, urges musicians to leave rap and rock and return to the original oriental dance music.

Rap music came onto the Egyptian scene in the late 1990s, and *Mahraganat*, also called Egyptian Electro, is a popular genre of street music that emerged in the late 2000s. Egyptians either love it or hate it, and it is subject to restrictions and disapproval by the Syndicate of Music Professions, despite its wide appeal.

Belly Dancing

This is the Western name for *Ra's Baladi* ("local dancing"), the sexy Middle Eastern dance that some historians believe

Ra's Baladi as an art form, performed on the concert stage.

was once a fertility ritual. The circular hip and arm movements mimic the emotions and rhythm of the music.

The Egyptians have a very conflicted relationship with belly dancing. On the one hand, they consider it a national art form and many families hire belly dancers to entertain at functions and wedding parties. Men, women, and children cheer on the dancer at such gatherings and encourage young girls to join her on the dance floor. At the same time, Egyptians certainly wouldn't encourage their daughters to be belly dancers.

FUN AND LEISURE

Egyptians certainly know how to enjoy their leisure time. Whether it's an evening out, a long weekend, or the summer vacation, there is a lot to offer the fun-seeker. Those who can afford it do travel abroad, but all Egyptians are proud of their own country and enjoy visiting their historical, cultural, and touristy spots. Since the coronavirus pandemic, niche travel options such as small private groups, desert experiences, ecotourism, and deeper cultural experiences have become more popular.

A Night Out

Egyptians work until quite late by Western standards as businesses and shops close at around 10:00 p.m., so people in the service industries might meet friends at a café or for a walk along the corniche in either Alexandria or Cairo. The last show at a cinema generally starts around 10.30 p.m. and this is a popular pastime.

Water Sports

With many cities and towns along the Nile or close to the Mediterranean or the Red Seas, there is a host of water sports to indulge in. One can sunbathe, swim, dive, and sail in the coastal cities and towns where the water temperatures are pleasant. The Nile offers sailing, fishing, and cruising.

Beaches

Egypt has some beautiful beaches on the north coast and on the Red Sea. Not all of these are accessible to the public, however, and a traveler couldn't simply stop their car at a beach and go for a swim, or snorkel or dive. Beaches, like hotels and resorts, are closed during the winter. There are designated public beaches and many private hotel or resort beaches, but not all have lifeguards.

Scuba divers in the Red Sea surrounded by a shoal of coral fish.

Tourists riding quad bikes in the eastern Egyptian desert.

Desert Leisure

The Egyptians enjoy their breathtakingly beautiful, if desolate, deserts, especially the star gazing. The main forms of desert activity are 4 x 4 desert safaris and sandboarding in the dunes. It is forbidden to pitch a tent at will, due to government restrictions on desert travel, especially in the northern parts of the Sinai, but camping tours to the desert can be arranged, generally with Bedouin tented accommodation.

Fishing

Fishing is a popular pastime—along the Nile, on Lake Nasser and other small lakes, and on the Mediterranean and Red Seas. Fishing boats can be chartered for deep sea fishing, but a permit is required, and foreigners will need to present their passports when getting it.

EATING OUT

There is nothing more appetizing than waking up to the smell of fresh coffee and baking, no matter where you are in the world. And in Egypt there are breakfast breads to delight every palate, from flaky croissants to *ai'sh baladi* (pita-like bread made with various flours). Contemporary Egyptian food is delicious. It is influenced by Turkish and Middle Eastern cuisine and has roots going back to the Ancient Egyptian diet. However, good Egyptian cooking is confined to the home, and in different houses one can expect to taste many variations of the same dish. Many restaurants serve Egyptian food, but the quality does not compare to home cooking. The good dishes found in homes require careful preparation, such as *mahshi* (rice stuffed vegetables), and restaurants tend to offer basic favorites that are easy to prepare such as *ful* and *falafel*.

Egyptians prefer to eat at home where they can be assured of their wife's or mother's hygiene and use of fresh ingredients and see no point in eating out when a perfectly good meal can be enjoyed at home.

As in Europe, food is considered part of the cultural heritage and today in Egypt some people are attempting to preserve traditional cooking techniques and recipes. However, an outsider is likely to taste only a fraction of genuine Egyptian cuisine. Most mid-range restaurants are decidedly uncreative, despite their excellent and witty names, and generally serve a variation of the same menu: pasta, burgers, wraps, and chicken dishes styled on Western favorites. Egyptian cuisine is not typically spicy, but Egyptians cook with huge amounts of ghee (clarified butter), so beware of heartburn. Dishes are usually accompanied by salads and pickles, and vegetables feature on most menus, but there are few vegetarian options.

The larger cities also have the well-known fast-food chains. Other eating establishments range from street stalls serving up affordable local food to exclusive restaurants offering steak, chicken, and pasta dishes. They are also expensive, which means that many Egyptians eat out mainly when they're in a hurry.

Throughout the country there are stalls or little shops serving Egyptian fast food. Many look uninviting, but don't be put off by first impressions: they are often clean and quick. However, street carts are not, by their nature, a hygienic option, as the food stays out in the sun too long and attracts flies.

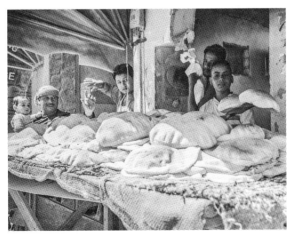

A street bakery in the oasis town of Siwa.

Ful and Ta'amiya (Felafel)

Along with bread, the indigenous fava bean, known locally as *ful*, supplies most Egyptians with their daily calorific intake. It is cooked in several ways, and everyone has their favorite. It can be cooked with ghee or olive oil; topped with *tahini* (sesame paste) or chopped tomatoes; sprinkled with cumin, or complemented with lemon. It can be served in pockets of *baladi* bread or served on a platter. *Ful* is nutritious and filling and usually eaten for breakfast.

Ful beans are also used to make falafel, known in Egypt as *ta'amiya*, one of the country's national dishes. This is a small ball or patty made from ground fava beans mixed with herbs and spices, then deep fried or baked. (Farther east, falafel is made with chickpeas rather than *ful*.)

Koshari

Koshari, made up of rice, noodles, lentils, tomato sauce, and fried onions, is a firm favorite among Egyptians. It is served in hole-in-the-wall shops, identifiable by their huge piles of rice and noodles in the window. Ordering is easy; you just shout out the number of portions you want. A little vinegar with garlic can be added for more flavor.

Molokhiyya

Molokhiyya, distinctively Egyptian, is a leafy green, summer vegetable cooked in chicken broth to make a thick soup. It can be served over rice with chicken or rabbit on the side, or on its own. *Molokhiyya* is seldom found in restaurants; and a domestic cook's talent is often measured by how good their *molokhiyya* is.

Mahshy, or *Dolma*: stuffed zucchini, eggplant, tomato, peppers, and vine leaves.

Koshari, the mixed-rice dish that is an Egyptian staple.

Meat

For the great majority of Egyptians meat is a luxury, and in most homes it is used in small quantities and served with vegetables or rice. However, restaurants specialize in meat dishes, especially grills.

A *kababgi* is a restaurant that serves Egyptian-style kebabs and other grills. A typical platter consists of *kabab*, *kofta* (minced lamb flavored with onions and spices), and lamb cutlets. When ordering, it is customary to order by the kilo (half a kilo is usually enough for two people). Grilled chicken is available widely and at certain restaurants an adventurous diner can try Egypt's national delicacy—pigeons stuffed with seasoned rice.

Fish

Fish is eaten everywhere. In the rural areas it is mainly river fish, which is considered inferior to saltwater fish from the Mediterranean. Some fish also comes from the Red Sea. Fish restaurants serve a straightforward barbecued grill or fish deep-fried in batter. You can pick the fish yourself at the restaurant ice buffet.

Fruits and Vegetables

The wide range of local fruits and vegetables are eaten in season, as imports are very expensive. If one's pocket allows, imported fruits and vegetables can be bought year-round at the upmarket supermarkets.

Vegetable stalls sell fresh fruit and vegetables. Because Egyptians buy for families, fruit vendors find it curious when foreigners ask for just one apple! Considered a poor man's fruit in Egypt, but a rare pop of deliciousness, is the gooseberry, available at a fraction of its cost abroad.

Desserts

Popular desserts include rice pudding infused with rose water. *Mahalabiya* is a white semolina-based pudding garnished with pistachios. *Om 'Ali* (mother of Ali) is a comforting bread pudding made with cooked pastry bits, milk, nuts, and spices. Also very common are oriental sweets such as baklava.

DELIVERIES

The food delivery service is quick and efficient, and ordering food in is something all city dwellers do. Every restaurant or café either delivers or customers can use the popular city delivery apps: some are region-specific, and some are national. (See apps on page 196.)

TABLE MANNERS

Most dining establishments in Egypt allow smoking and it is difficult to find a nonsmoking restaurant, so nonsmokers might like to sit near an open window or choose a well-ventilated restaurant or café.

Bread is eaten with every meal and, when eating a stew or a dip, it is normal to use pita bread in place of cutlery. Starters and dips are often eaten communally: everyone dips their bread into the same plate. Knives and forks can be requested and will be provided.

As we have seen, if invited out for a meal, it is polite to insist on paying. This can end up in a long back and forth and the person with the strongest will usually pays. It is courteous to return the invitation.

THE *AHWA*

The *ahwa*, the traditional Egyptian coffee shop, is the social hub of most Egyptian males. It is where men meet, talk, and unwind, where politics and society are discussed, theories formulated, and rumors spread. Men go there after work to shed the day's tension over a game of backgammon or by smoking a *shisha* (water pipe). The *shisha* is more than just a nicotine fix; it is a social affair that should not be hurried.

Each neighborhood is dotted with *ahawi* (the plural of *ahwa*). Some are more rustic than others, some more polished, but all are fairly basic as far as interiors go. They consist of an indoor section with tables and chairs that overflow onto the sidewalk. An *ahwa* has a loyal clientele.

Unwinding at the *ahwa*, Cairo.

The menu is limited to tea, coffee, and a variety of other hot or cold drinks. While women are not actually banned from entering, a traditional *ahwa* is a man's place. There are several *ahawi* that welcome women, but these are mainly aimed at tourists.

DRINKING

Coffee
Turkish coffee is traditionally the coffee drunk in Egypt, although there are many European-style cafés that serve cappuccinos and lattes.

The traditional cup of coffee is thick and strong. It is made from finely ground coffee beans, infused with cardamom, and brewed in a small pot. The coffee is not filtered, so, when served in little cups, the grains sink to

Traditional coffee being served.

the bottom. Because the sugar is mixed in with the coffee prior to brewing, you should specify the level of sweetness required when ordering it. *Ahwa sada* means coffee without sugar, *ahwa 'ariha* contains little sugar, *ahwa mazbuta* has a little more sugar, *ahwa ziada* is sweet, and *ahwa caramel* is very sweet.

Tea

Egyptians are avid *shay* (tea) drinkers. Dried tea leaves are boiled in water over a stove, which makes the cup a lot stronger than tea bags. Egyptians drink their tea sweet. If you order tea in an *ahwa*, it will usually be served with sugar so it's best to say upfront if you don't want sugar, or to avoid stirring until you've tasted it. A refreshing drink is mint tea, where sprigs of fresh mint are added to the tea.

Tea is served in glasses in most establishments, but cafés that cater to the tourist market may serve it in a cup. Tea with milk is generally a breakfast drink and will be made with boiled milk rather than boiled water.

Other Hot Drinks

Egyptians enjoy herbal teas such as hibiscus, aniseed, cinnamon, and caraway. These are the drink of choice when they have consumed all the caffeine they can tolerate for a day. *Sahlab* is a milky drink made from orchid bulbs and served with nuts and cinnamon. In the winter, Egyptians love *hommos el sham*, a thin soup of chickpea and chili that is treated as a hot drink and served in a glass, which warms one to the core.

Cold Drinks

Fruit juice stands are one of Egypt's real delights. In the summer, people bunch around shops and stands that blend fresh juices and juice cocktails. The most popular is sugarcane juice, a great pick-me-up, especially in the summer heat. Also on offer are mouthwatering combinations of strawberry, mango, banana, and orange. Sugar is always added for the Egyptian sweet tooth, so if you don't want sugar, just ask.

Other cold drinks include *'er soos* (licorice) and *tamr hindi* (tamarind), *karkady* (hibiscus), and *sobia* (a sweet rice and coconut dairy drink). During Ramadan a much wider range of delicious cold drinks is available.

Alcohol

While Islam prohibits the consumption of alcohol, in practice some Muslims do drink, and Egyptian Christians and foreigners are, of course, free to do so.

Egypt has a growing wine industry. Beer is also produced locally: Stella, a light lager, is the most popular brand. International brands of beer, wine, and spirits are available in high-end restaurants and hotels that cater to a foreign clientele; however, bars are few and between. Unless imported, avoid spirits as they typically don't taste anything like the competing foreign brands.

Alcohol can be bought at liquor stores in all but the most conservative cities. Imported beer, wine, and spirits are available but expensive.

BARS AND NIGHTCLUBS

Egyptian nightlife is as multifaceted as its society. From the seedy bars of Cairo's Pyramids Road with their belly dancers and Arabic music to the swanky, shiny nightclubs of Sharm el Sheikh, Egypt has it all.

It is sometimes difficult to remember that Egypt is a conservative society when you step into the voguish bars and nightclubs that dot the large cities. Hidden from society's restrictive rules, the wealthy and the Westernized drink and party the night away behind closed doors.

In Cairo and Alexandria, bars that once catered mainly to the expatriate community now play host to a clientele of foreigners and locals. They are a bit rough around the edges but have a nostalgic feel lacking in the smarter places.

When an Egyptian refers to a "cabaret," he is probably referring to a nightclub that has dinner, drinks, and a belly dance show. Traditional Egyptians consider these places to be little more than institutionalized brothels and may not be as keen as foreigners to spend an evening at a cabaret.

TIPPING

Egyptians earn much less than people in the West and many depend on *ba'shish* (tips). A tip is not seen as a reward for exceptional service, but as a regular small supplement. Someone who carries your bags expects a tip, as does the parking attendant who helps you park your car, and the usher who shows you to your seat in the cinema. For *ba'shish*, your butcher will get you better meat from the back of the shop, and your doorman will run errands for you. Wealthy Egyptians tip their way through most things.

The restaurant check includes the price of your meal, the general sales tax, and a gratuity fee. The latter should not be confused with a tip to the waitstaff though; it is a tax that all restaurants pay to the government. If you would like to leave a tip add it to the bill, otherwise your server won't receive anything at all. Ten percent is recommended—a little more is always welcome.

In the new metered taxis, tips are no longer expected, although often people do round up the fare (see page 159).

SPORTS

In Egypt sports is synonymous with football (soccer). Egyptians are football crazy and many streets are turned into football pitches in the summer, regardless of traffic.

Every city has its own social club (the bigger cities have several) where children go to train in their chosen sport. It is also a meeting place for families, and many have their Friday lunches there.

Football fever sweeps the country after international wins, with people celebrating on the streets wearing Egypt's colors—black, white, and red. The two main Cairo teams, Ahly and Zamalek, attract the greatest support and rivalry between them is fierce. Egypt is the most successful African football champion, having won the Africa Cup of Nations seven times between 1986 and 2010. Regrettably, since recent stadia skirmishes, attendance at matches has been limited to a handful of people with club connections—a big blow to fans. Nevertheless, they still support their teams by watching televised matches at cafés or at home with friends.

On an international level, Egyptians have excelled at handball and squash. There are twenty-four golf courses, including some of the best in the MENA region. Green fees for non-residents range from 100 to 200 EGP.

OUT OF TOWN

On national holidays, religious feasts, and long weekends, the Egyptians head for the coast. Day trips to Alexandria and the Mediterranean beaches are popular family outings. Those who can afford it have second homes on the north coast or in southern Sinai and the Red Sea resorts, and spend their summer weekends away from the city. At these times local public beaches are packed with revelers, and travelers who don't like crowds should avoid them.

CHAPTER SEVEN

TRAVEL, HEALTH, & SAFETY

Egypt is a traveler's treasure trove, with its renowned archaeological sites, beaches, and deserts. But it is also overcrowded and polluted. Most tourists are shielded from this reality by organized tour companies, and are taken from site to restaurant without having to brave the Egypt that Egyptians experience daily. If you are traveling independently, however, it is important to be aware of the law (that is, where foreigners may or may not travel and who they may or may not travel alone with), road etiquette, and health and safety hazards.

ROADS AND TRAFFIC

A bird's-eye view of one of Egypt's main city squares would appear to show an utterly chaotic, crowded, and frenetic scene. On the ground, foreign visitors find the melee confusing, but Egyptians understand the system within this chaos. Pedestrians, carts, and animals weave through cars in a calculated tango. There exists a sort of Driving Darwinism, a survival of the fittest in which timid drivers do not fare well. And while there is tension on the streets, this rarely turns into aggression. Most of the time, the stress is defused by a little humor and a lot of patience.

Driving

Driving in Egypt is stressful, but foreigners often remark that being a passenger is far scarier than being a driver; at least, when driving, you exercise a degree of control.

Egyptian drivers may gesticulate with impatience, but this is usually just venting, as most drivers are considerate in allowing other motorists to cross in front of them or take their place in a long line of traffic. Western rules concerning right of way, signaling, and use of mirrors do not apply here. Lanes are disregarded, with sometimes as many as four cars side by side in a two-lane street. Side view mirrors are folded in to save space, and many cars lose their side mirrors. Cars cut in front of one another regularly and everyone always seems to be in a rush. And then there is the use of the horn. A foreigner has trouble deciphering its meaning: sometimes it means "hurry up," sometimes "be careful," and sometimes it is used to greet other drivers. Since there are no stop signs or traffic lights in the suburbs, drivers typically honk as they approach an intersection, and this constant honking can be disconcerting for travelers. Drivers who flash their headlights are warning you to stay out of their way. Traffic lights are frequently ignored. Often, there will be a traffic policeman at the main junctions to direct the traffic. So, what does a newcomer do when faced with such challenges?

The golden rule is to find an Egyptian to cross with. Stick as close to them as possible, look ahead, worry about what's in front of you, not what's behind you, and don't be intimidated by other drivers beeping at you. But of course, have your wits about you.

Despite attempts at improvement, many areas still have inadequate roads with poor paving, potholes, and poor signage. Intercity roads are generally in good condition but rural mud roads can challenge the best of drivers.

Speed limits are taken seriously, especially on intercity superhighways, where distance-controlled radar equipment picks up speeding drivers. If you are caught speeding your license will be confiscated and you will have to go to traffic headquarters to pay a fine to retrieve it—a long and bureaucratic process that is best avoided. On the road, motorists have an "us vs. them" attitude toward the police. They show solidarity by flashing their headlights at oncoming traffic to warn motorists to slow down if radar is in operation or traffic police are manning a roadblock.

For offenses such as talking on your cell phone while driving, not wearing a seat belt, or parking where forbidden (especially along the corniches in the coastal or riverside cities), you may have your license confiscated. In such instances many Egyptians pay the traffic policeman to "forget" the incident. Never under any circumstance will an *officer* accept such a bribe, so don't offer money to anyone with stars on their lapels! However, foreigners are strongly advised to stay on the right side of the law.

An international driver's license is valid for one year. Foreigners can also use their home licenses for up to three months. Residents can apply for an Egyptian license. Make sure you always have ID papers, driver's license, and registration papers on you as there are regular checkpoints where you will be asked to produce this documentation.

Parking

Motorists can park in most places except in front of government buildings, embassies, and diplomats' and politicians' residences. Signage is not always very clear. Usually the best approach is: if another non-official car is parked there, you can probably park there too, but try and ask one of the *bowabs* (doormen) in the area. When a parking space is particularly tight and it's difficult to negotiate the space, passersby or *bowabs* will typically offer to park the car for you or guide you—yet another aspect of the Egyptians' innate helpfulness.

The upside is that street parking is free. The downside is the difficulty of finding a parking space, especially in high density areas. Egyptians have mastered the art of parallel parking, squeezing into the most unlikely gaps. In the cities, and particularly in Cairo, a degree of creativity must be used. Although double-parking is illegal, it is very common and rarely attracts police attention. If you are double-parking, do not set your emergency brake and keep your wheels aligned. A driver whose car you have blocked will push your car out of the way. So do not be shocked when you come out to find your car slightly shifted from its original spot, or a random stranger pushing it. He is probably not trying to steal it.

In most central areas, a parking attendant, called a *sayis*, is there to find you a parking spot and help you fit into it, for a small fee. Sometimes, people give their keys to the *sayis*, who will find a parking spot for them. Not every *sayis* is an employee of the state. Some wear badges, some are hired by restaurants or popular establishments for their clientele, and some work freelance, but all are treated equally by Egyptians whether they are official or not.

Accidents

An accident must be reported at a police station if a driver wants to file an insurance claim. The number of people covered by insurance is low. Uninsured drivers who have crashed into each other prefer to settle the dispute on the spot without resorting to the system, providing there are no injuries and no serious damage. Status and wealth play a part here; if there is serious damage and the person at fault is richer (drives a better car), they will probably pay for it. Settlement really depends on the drivers. Very often, if there is no serious damage, people will get out of their cars, make a little fuss, and then go their own way.

Pedestrians

Drivers are not the only ones who need to display a little feistiness; pedestrians must also show a fair share. Smooth sidewalks are practically nonexistent. Walking in Egypt, particularly in Cairo, is like being on a mini assault course. Sidewalks are rudely interrupted by litter, parked cars, holes, pipes, and electrical wires. Sensible closed walking shoes should be worn for outside use; high heels are strictly for indoors.

Crossing a busy street poses one of the most difficult challenges and newcomers have been known to take a cab across a square rather than face it. Pedestrian crossings are ignored by traffic, unless manned by a traffic policeman. Black-and-white stripes across a street do not, in practice, mean right of way for pedestrians.

Assertion and even aggression are required. Waiting for cars to slow down can leave you by the side of the road indefinitely. You need to be focused. Take that first step and cross. Stop in the middle of the road if you feel a car is coming too fast; let it pass and move to the next lane. If you hesitate and go back and forth, you are likely to be knocked over. If it all gets too much, find a group of Egyptians and cross with them. Eventually, you will know how to walk the walk.

LOCAL TRANSPORTATION

Public transportation is used mainly by the working class and students. The wealthy rarely use it, except perhaps when traveling between cities. Egyptians are curious about foreigners on a journey and will use the opportunity to strike up a conversation and ask about the world beyond their borders. If spoken to, it is polite to answer. If an interesting conversation is struck up, you may even be invited for a glass of tea.

The Metro and Trams

Cairo's rapid transit system, the Cairo Metro, operates from 5:00 a.m. to 1:00 a.m., except during Ramadan when the last train runs at 2:00 a.m. It is the fastest and cheapest way to travel. The lines run across 74 stations on three operational routes, numbered 1 to 3. The Metro

Cairo Metro carriage for women only.

is clean and efficient. The blue signs at all stations signify the position of the cars reserved for women only, although women are free to use all the cars.

Cairo and Alexandria both have tram networks. In Cairo, the system is limited to the northwestern Heliopolis district. In Alexandria, the network is extensive, and the system is a reliable, cheap, and extremely efficient way of getting around the city, especially when roads are choked by traffic congestion.

Municipal Buses
Standard-sized municipal buses are available in all the main cities, but are mainly used by local residents.

Microbuses
The most widely used kind of bus is the microbus, which seats about fourteen people and has fixed routes and fixed

fares; however, it is not easy for the uninitiated foreigner to know exactly what these are as they operate both within and between cities. Usually someone at the door calls out the destination; this is also the person who collects the money. If there is no one on the door, then it is customary to pass the fare forward, and the front seat passenger becomes the designated conductor. You can get on and off where you want. Simply hail one anywhere along the route and get on.

Microbus drivers are infamous for their reckless driving, so do not expect a smooth ride.

Minibuses

Twelve-seater minibuses, smaller than microbuses, can be overcrowded during rush hour in the main cities, and hardly ever come to a complete halt, except in a traffic jam. Passengers pack themselves in, leaving hardly any room to maneuver. Pickpocketing is a risk.

Passengers boarding a microbus during the afternoon rush hour.

There are also airconditioned minibus services in the main cities, which are slightly more expensive than normal buses but less crowded. Standing is not allowed, and the bus will only start moving once all the seats have been filled.

Taxis and Uber

This is the most convenient way to travel. There are plenty of taxis and fares are the same as an Uber ride. Taxis can be hailed anywhere on the street, but the Uber app is required to order a ride. Recently introduced white taxis have replaced the older black and white cabs in Cairo (yellow and black in Alexandria) and offer air conditioning and meters. This has removed the hassle of bargaining over the fare. Old taxis are still operational.

Tipping is not generally expected in metered taxis and Uber rides, but people often round up the fare. So if your fare was seventeen Egyptian pounds you'd probably pay twenty. A tip of five Egyptian pounds and up, depending on the length of the journey, will always be welcome.

Taxi drivers may decline to accept payment of the fare, and what seems like a courteous gesture is not a genuine offer—it is expected that you will insist, after which payment will be accepted. The reason for this may be that if they name a fee, it might be lower than you're willing to pay.

The high rate of unemployment has meant that many educated men resort to working as cab drivers. Some have rudimentary English and understand simple directions. Others, particularly those in the tourist areas, will surprise you with their command of the language.

Taxi and Uber drivers love to chat, especially with foreigners. It is common for a driver to act as an unofficial tour guide, pointing out important buildings and monuments. Politics is their favorite topic, and they often expect Western passengers to explain their countries' foreign policies vis-à-vis the Middle East. It is up to you as to how far to engage in such conversations; putting on a pair of sunglasses or busying yourself on your phone can cut out unwanted conversation or attention.

It is normal for a cab driver to take on other passengers during the rush hour, but unlikely for them to do so if they are driving a foreigner. If they do, and you are in a hurry, you can ask not to have other passengers on board or to be dropped off first.

Women should always try to sit in the back of the cab, especially if they are alone. It is uncomfortable for the driver to have a strange woman sitting close to him in the front if she is the only passenger, but fully acceptable if you're part of a group.

Drivers who own their own vehicles consider their car their little space in the world and put great effort into personalizing it. Family photos on the dashboard and religious symbols hanging from the mirror are typical, or even stuffed toys and mini chandeliers.

All drivers have cell phones. If you have established a relationship with a driver, you can arrange to be dropped off at, and picked up from, appointments.

INTERCITY TRAVEL

There are many options for intercity travel throughout Egypt, suitable for both the budget and the luxury traveler.

Tourist police may stop foreigners and ask where they are from and where they are headed. Do not be alarmed—this is standard procedure. Tourists' safety is their responsibility and they take it seriously.

Air Travel

EgyptAir and a variety of charter airlines operate flights between cities and most neighboring countries. A passport is not required for travel inside Egypt—usually any form of ID with a picture will do (though a passport will be needed at a hotel and for international arrivals and departures). Prices on EgyptAir vary, so it is worth asking your booking agent for the cheapest available fare, or making the booking on the EgyptAir website.

Buses

A variety of bus companies connects most cities and towns in Egypt. If your destination is off the beaten path, then expect to take a bus to the nearest major city and hire a driver for the balance of the trip and expect to pay premium. Tickets can be bought on the vendors' websites and at the bus station, and sometimes on the bus.

The description "Deluxe air-conditioned buses" in no way guarantees luxury travel (even if the brochure promises that). At best, you will have a designated seat, relatively clean toilets on board, and restroom and convenience store snack stops en route. Sleeping can prove difficult as the onboard entertainment tends to be a loud Egyptian film on a screen at the front of the bus, or religious music, depending on the driver. Travel with earplugs or headphones if you find noise an annoyance.

Sometimes non-air-conditioned buses are unavoidable, and the experience is altogether different. While seats may be designated, packs of people traveling together, sometimes whole families, will want to sit together. There will be a lot of commotion on the trip, with people and their belongings taking up space and air.

Trains

Like most things in Egypt, trains are defined by price and type of traveler. The more direct trains cost more and are mainly used by tourists and affluent Egyptians. They have comfortable, air-conditioned, first-class carriages. Second class is also comfortable, but not always air-conditioned. In third class the seats are not padded, and the carriages can be overcrowded and uncomfortable on long journeys.

A fast train between Alexandria and Cairo has been introduced. Foreigners should be aware that they are expected to pay their fares in US dollars and will not be allowed to purchase a ticket using local currency.

Sleepers are available to places such as Luxor and Aswan in the south of Egypt.

WHERE TO STAY

Hotels and Airbnbs

Egypt has accommodation to suit every budget. Prices are rarely negotiable—never in the top- and middle-range hotels. Egyptians need ID to stay at a hotel and foreigners must show their passports. A foreigner checking in with an Egyptian of the opposite sex will be asked to produce a marriage certificate. Airbnbs are typically owned by Egyptians and the above rule is applicable here too. Very many owners state that their accommodation is for families only—this means not only a couple with their children, it also subtly means no unmarried Egyptian–foreigner combo. While a foreign woman may stand a (very) small chance of sharing a room with her Egyptian boyfriend, an Egyptian woman will most certainly not be indulged similarly, and in fact some Egyptian women may be turned away even when trying to book two rooms, which arouses suspicions. Hotel management simply don't want the headache of dealing with the authorities if they are found to be hosting a couple breaking the law. It is best not to place yourself in the situation as it is illegal for men and women to share a room unless they are married.

Apartments

Finding an apartment in the metropolitan cities is easy. Once you've settled on the area you'd like to live in, you can either approach an agent at a reputable realtor or you can identify an apartment block you like the look of and find the *bowab* (see page 121). He knows the availability of apartments and will be able to introduce you to the landlord. If he warms to you, he might offer to negotiate for you. Once the lease has been signed, give him a small gratuity. The landlord will also be paying him for finding a tenant. Establish a good relationship with your *bowab*—you will need him later. Two months' deposit plus a month's rental in advance is required for a furnished apartment, while a single month's deposit plus the rental is required for an unfurnished apartment.

Before agreeing to take an apartment, it is wise to assess the noise level of the surrounding area. Mosques broadcast the call to prayer five times a day starting at sunrise. While this can be a beautiful experience, you may not want it coming through a loudspeaker right into your bedroom. Schools sing the national anthem and put out daily digests on a loudspeaker. People do get used to it, and you know you have reached local status once you manage to sleep through the morning sounds. However, if you are a light sleeper, this is something to be aware of.

If you don't like the furniture in a furnished apartment, focus on whether the place is clean, and has good working appliances and a working landline. The landlord can store the furniture.

Landlords are required by law to register the lease at a designated government office. Both parties are expected to sign two top copies; each retains a signed copy and the office retains a stamped copy. While it's best to try to insist on a legal lease to protect yourself in case of a dispute, some landlords are unwilling to pay the tax the lease attracts and will resist registering. If this happens, the lessee seldom has any recourse.

When the contract for a lease is signed, don't be surprised if the rent stated in the paperwork is lower than the rent you've agreed to pay. It helps the landlord avoid tax and doesn't affect you. Just because you have a lease, though, doesn't mean that the terms will be honored, especially if you're still in residence when summer comes. Many a landlord has been known to plead difficult circumstances and a need to vacate the apartment you're renting, when in fact he can earn double or triple what you're paying during the summer season. Occupancy tussles can turn unpleasant, and it's probably best to cut your losses and move elsewhere.

HEALTH

No vaccines are prescribed for travel to Egypt; however, because of the high rate of Hepatitis-C in the country, vaccination against this is recommended. Do this well in advance, as the vaccine is a three-dose regimen.

There are a few ways to minimize sickness during your stay in Egypt. Choose bottled water over tap water in areas with poor infrastructure. Ask for drinks without ice cubes. Avoid undercooked meat on street stalls, and meat from unknown eating establishments. Salad needs to be very well washed in clean water. If buying sandwiches on the street, specify that you don't want salad.

Foreigners should avoid taking a dip in the Nile. The river is a habitat for the bilharzia parasite that causes the chronic disease schistosomiasis. Symptoms include muscle pains, diarrhea, fever, vomiting, coughing, and blood in the urine. It is treatable with medication.

Egyptian doctors are well trained, but hygiene in many public hospitals is questionable and nurses are inexpert. In nonemergency situations, private clinics are the best option. Most of the time these operate on a first-come first-served basis and the doctors are likely to speak English. With better-known consultants, an appointment is required. Private hospitals are excellent, with highly trained staff and well-maintained facilities.

SAFETY

Terrorism

Protective of its tourist industry, the government has enforced strict measures to minimize any threat to it. There are metal detectors at the entries of all tourist sites and hotels. Police are present at all spots frequented by foreigners, and undercover police are always present as an extra precaution. In a global context, Egypt is not a greater terrorist target than any other country vulnerable to insurgents. North Sinai is heavily guarded and patrolled to avoid infiltration by any terrorists who may consider it to be an easy entry point.

Crime

By international standards, Egypt is a safe country. Random violence is rare, and visitors often mention how safe they feel walking around. As in any major tourist area elsewhere, pickpocketing and petty crime exists.

After the 2011 uprising, when the police disappeared from the streets, crime spiked temporarily, with an increase in robberies and carjackings, particularly on the highways leading to Cairo's suburbs. However, even though policing is now at full capacity, it is wise to exercise the sort of reasonable caution expected in most large cities.

Sinai remains the most insecure part of the country, and there is a strong military presence in the northern part of the peninsula to root out militant groups and smugglers.

The southern coasts of the peninsula, where most of the luxury beach resorts are concentrated, are largely unaffected, but again, sensible precautions are advised.

Women

Foreign women are often misunderstood in this conservative society. Friendly conduct can be interpreted as flirtation, and women out at night without a male companion can give the impression that they are inviting attention. For these reasons foreign women may attract unwanted attention on the streets. Most Egyptian women dress modestly to conservatively when out in public. They do not show legs, bare arms, or cleavage and it is advisable to follow their example to avoid harassment. If you are going to a Western-style establishment where it is acceptable to wear revealing clothes, wear a large shawl or a coat on the journey there and back. Abiding by these rules can help minimize, but not always eliminate, unpleasant experiences.

Most annoying behavior takes the form of whistling and leering, but if it extends to groping this is most definitely harassment and should be reported to the police. Some guidebooks advise women to turn round and shout at the aggressor in Arabic, but this is unwise. It will not shame anyone into stopping and might in fact provoke laughter and possibly more harassment. A woman should not interact with the aggressor. She can either shout out loudly, which will draw enough attention to scare the offender away, or walk away from the situation. Interacting with the harasser one-on-one is unfortunately a no-win situation for a foreign woman. Harassment rarely takes place at tourist resorts and beaches, where people are used to mingling with foreigners.

CHAPTER EIGHT

BUSINESS BRIEFING

Foreign businesspeople are often surprised by the coexistence of modern technology and antiquated business practices in Egypt. Older establishments, with their bureaucracy and officialdom, exist alongside an increasing number of modern enterprises and multinational companies.

Sadat's Open Door Policy started the move toward a free market economy. In 2004, the cabinet took major steps to streamline and liberalize the economy, including faster-paced privatization, customs reforms, liberalization of the banking industry, and the active encouragement of private enterprise. Because liberalization is still ongoing, and the law is being amended continuously, it is essential to seek professional advice to keep up with the latest rules and regulations. Government websites also provide up-to-date information.

The big cities have excellent business facilities. Business centers and rooms at major hotels are equipped with satellite television, fax, printing facilities, and wireless internet connections.

In general the pace of business is slower in Egypt than in the West. The traditional management style is top–down, with the head of a company acting as the decision-maker. Trust is vital to any activity, and it takes time to create networks and establish personal relationships.

THE BUSINESS LANDSCAPE

The Egyptian business landscape is varied and changing rapidly. There are still government-owned institutions. The number of family businesses is decreasing, as children and siblings choose to break away from hereditary careers or business structures and move to personally chosen fields. Multinational companies are on the increase as legislation has made the environment more favorable for investment; however, due to complicated foreign currency controls, it is wise to arrange for the payment of foreign nationals in their home country bank accounts. There are also many small- and medium-sized companies.

Foreigners wishing to do business in Egypt can establish a presence in three ways. They set up a Limited Liability Company, a Limited Shares Company, or a Joint Stock Company. Alternatively, a representation or branch office can be set up. A local partner, while not required by law, can help penetrate the market, cut through red tape, and untangle the web of bribes and sweeteners. The law requires that an Egyptian agent be used when submitting a tender to a public sector company, but not when dealing with the Ministry of Defense.

WORKING DAYS

All businesses are closed on Friday, the Muslim holy day. Private businesses tend to have a five-day workweek, from Sunday to Thursday, but many firms work on Saturdays. Hours are from 9:00 a.m. to 5:00 p.m., although smaller businesses start later and may close at 7:00 or 8.00 p.m.

Government ministries and offices and banks do not operate on Fridays. The government sector works six days a week, from Saturday to Thursday, generally from 8:00 a.m. to 2:00 p.m. Trade unions are closely controlled by the state and independent trade union movements are still campaigning for reforms.

Embassies don't open on Fridays and usually not on Saturdays. Companies closed on Fridays may take Saturday off too. Although Sunday is not an official day of rest, non-governmental institutions and warehouses and craftsmen may well not be open for business on this day. Check opening hours by calling in advance rather than relying on website information that may not have been updated. Barbershops, hairdressers, and beauty salons do not operate on Mondays, but stay open on Fridays, Saturdays, and Sundays to take advantage of their customers' days off.

BUREAUCRACY

Despite the reforms aimed at cutting red tape, Egypt still suffers from practices inherited from the bureaucratic past. Red tape is an unavoidable and frustrating aspect of life encountered in all official transactions, such as opening bank accounts, signing work contracts, extending visas, and gaining residency as a foreigner.

Some prospective employers will attend to the documentation for a specific job as the requirements are always changing, but you should prepare by bringing official copies of your personal and professional documents. It is advisable to keep the originals of these in your own possession at all times. It is essential to obtain official copies of everything you sign—your apartment lease, banking documents, or your work contracts. The Egyptians take the red tape and the long lines in government departments in their stride, and think nothing of pushing to the front of the line and being quite surprised at anyone's annoyance. Expect the Egyptian officials' moods to range from indifference to brusqueness, to friendliness, but in all cases treat them respectfully and you will find them relatively cooperative.

It is best to visit the Egyptian embassy in your country beforehand to ascertain precisely what is required for tourist, investment, or working visas.

BUSINESS CULTURE

Business success depends greatly on connections. Good personal relationships and trust are needed to initiate new ventures and to ensure the smooth running of existing arrangements. A pleasant rapport paves the way for payments to be made on time, appointments to be honored, and mistakes to be corrected swiftly. Networking is an essential part of business life, and socializing can take place during working hours and in the workweek.

In Egypt, things take time, a factor that has frustrated many a foreign visitor. Major decisions are made at the highest level, with subordinates in charge of initiating business and following up with logistics. Egyptians do not naturally delegate. The more junior the contact, the longer it takes for matters to move forward, as each employee waits for the green light from his senior. Bureaucracy also slows things down, particularly when dealing with government departments.

TIME IS NOT MONEY

A foreign executive came to Egypt on private business. He hired an Egyptian advisor to assist him, who arranged a meeting with an Egyptian businessman at the latter's home. Everyone sat down in the formal seating area.

The Egyptian wanted to talk generally and get to know the foreigner before addressing matters of substance. He offered tea and an array of cakes and pastries, and the best china was brought out for the occasion. The foreigner, not wishing to waste his host's time, declined to eat and tried to push on with the subject of his business.

At the end of the meeting the foreigner left frustrated because little had been discussed, and the Egyptian felt that his hospitality had been snubbed. He called the advisor and asked him not arrange any more meetings with the foreigner.

Understanding the Egyptian pace, and working with it rather than against it, will determine success or failure. When problems arise, the only way to solve them is by remaining calm and proceeding with patience. Expressing annoyance and issuing ultimatums will not only have a negative effect, it may end the deal altogether. Egyptians will put their pride before their interest. If they feel insulted or patronized, they would rather cease negotiations and take their business elsewhere.

When making a complaint, it is important to direct it to the decision-maker, usually the business owner or managing director. Addressing major complaints to subordinates will fall on deaf ears.

Knowledge of English among Egyptian businesspeople should not be assumed. Often, the heads of large companies will belong to the more affluent Westernized classes who are likely to speak English. This is not necessarily the case with middle management and government officials, so it is wise to find a translator if you do not already have a local agent.

"SWEETENERS"

High-level corruption is openly discussed in the Egyptian media, and fighting it is a declared government policy. Several prominent businessmen and public officials have been prosecuted and jailed following corruption scandals. However, low-level corruption is endemic. "Sweeteners" in their many forms are often the price to pay for business. It is a notion that has become deeply woven into the fabric of Egyptian commerce. Bribery and corruption are common in small- and medium-sized businesses and when dealing with the public sector and government ministries. In the private sector bribery is rare, although invoices can be overstated with the unspoken consent of the other party. That said, there are many employees or officials who would be insulted to be offered a bribe.

While large businesses and multinational companies have strict codes of conduct and ethics, they are sometimes obliged to abide by the unspoken rules and turn a blind eye to low-level bribes, or engage in excessive gift giving.

Generally, to get something done, a string of licenses, clearances, and permits needs to be obtained. Some form of bribery is expected at many of these bureaucratic junctions. At this level and in the short term, everyone involved seems to benefit from the practice. The excuse made is that they are helping underpaid functionaries with extra cash in return for speeding up paperwork. And on their part, the functionaries feel that the privileged business elite can afford to part with their cash, so why not? Many depend on bribes to supplement inadequate salaries; for others it has simply become part of the culture. It is advisable not to indulge in bribery, which is illegal, and, if discovered, penalties can be severe for the law breaker.

"EGYPTIAN STANDARD TIME"

Most appointments start late in Egypt, and people tend to be tardy due to traffic congestion, which is highly unpredictable. Rush hours, of course, play a part, but road accidents—which are very common—can create bottlenecks that take hours to unblock. Dignitaries and senior government officials traveling by car also cause immense traffic backlogs, as streets are usually sealed off when they are traveling on the road.

Foreigners are known and expected to be more punctual, and Egyptians will make special efforts to be on time when meeting them. Visitors should try to show up on time but should not expect their contact to be punctual. If you are running behind, it is polite to phone the contact and advise them. To be realistic, one should limit the number of fixed appointments to one or two a day.

BUSINESS ETIQUETTE

Respect

Status and seniority are especially evident in the business environment. Most communications will be formal at first. Addressing someone by their correct title honors that formality and shows respect. It is crucial to ascertain a business contact's correct title prior to a meeting. A minister, for example, should be addressed as "Your Excellency." Anyone with a doctorate expects to be called "Doctor," and an engineer as "Engineer." Failure to observe these niceties comes across as disrespect or arrogance, a trait that Egyptians dislike intensely.

Most Egyptians should be addressed by their title and their given name: a Mohammed Hanafi should be addressed as *Ustaz* Mohammed or *Doktoor* Mohammed. Some Egyptians, particularly in the services and tourist industries, also use the English title of Mister, so *Mr*

Mohammed is also acceptable. In writing, use the title and the person's full name: *Ustaz Mohammed Hanafi*. It is useful to find out before the meeting how to write your contact's name in English, to facilitate correct pronunciation.

Business Dress

When it comes to business dress, visitors are expected to observe Egyptian standards of modesty. Men should wear suits and ties to formal or first meetings. Shirts and smart trousers are acceptable at informal meetings, while jeans and T-shirts are never acceptable. Long hair, piercings, or any visible jewelry—other than a wedding ring—are considered unprofessional.

Women should dress conservatively in a business context. It is essential to avoid body-hugging outfits or low necklines. Skirts should be long enough to fall below the knee when sitting down. Trouser suits are the safest option.

Business Cards

Business cards are the must-have accessory and are exchanged on every possible occasion. They can be printed quickly and cheaply in Egypt, and it is considered a nice touch to have them printed in both English and Arabic.

Business Gifts

Gifts are usually exchanged at the end of the year. They are offered to contacts with whom you have developed a professional relationship or with whom you wish to do so. Appropriate gifts include elegant stationery or crafts from your own country. Do not be extravagant as this pressures your contact into returning a gift of the same value.

MEETINGS

When arranging a meeting, it is best to book it well ahead and confirm it closer to the date. First meetings will be very formal affairs, generally at a place of business. Formal dress and formal forms of address are required. Address your contacts by title and first name until they suggest otherwise.

Despite this degree of formality, meetings are also personal occasions, so it is considered rude to walk in and get straight down to business. Even first meetings begin with tea or coffee and some conversation on topics such as culture, history, and sports. Avoid subjects such as religion, politics, and the Arab–Israeli conflict. If a relationship has already been developed with the contact, it is appropriate to ask about health and family. When referring to family, however, speak generally, and do not ask about a wife or a daughter specifically.

Unlike presentations (see below), meetings involve animated dialogue that may seem to dip in and out of the subject quite aimlessly. There may also be bullet point discussions, depending on the situation. Expect meetings to be patchy, with many disruptions, tea, and more tea. Remain focused, ignore the distractions, and be patient. Egyptians love talking and use the occasion to try to impress, often by trumpeting their personal achievements. Don't worry. This is only a way of getting down to business, and don't look at your watch, as this is considered rude. Use the time to get to know your contact. Ask questions, but avoid personal topics.

After the first meeting, it is very important to follow up with phone calls, to make sure that the business is progressing, to keep the lines of communication open, and to have a personal talk with the other party.

After several communications, your contact may suggest moving the meeting from the office to a café or a less formal setting. This indicates that you have moved up the confidence ladder and the relationship is developing.

Never leave a meeting on a purely business note; rather make another few minutes of social talk.

DEALING WITH THE GOVERNMENT

The government exercises a great deal of control over the business environment. It appoints boards of directors of public sector corporations or companies that are partly state owned. Sometimes, it will not put a tender out to public bidding but will appoint a particular company to take the job. Chairmen of privately owned companies network closely with ministers.

When negotiating with the government, remember that things can be vetoed from the top. There is little transparency, and one can be subject to arbitrary decisions at any stage before signing a contract.

PRESENTATIONS

Egyptians tend to prefer meetings to presentations because they like to participate actively, rather than just listen passively. However, formal presentations are becoming increasingly common as new technologies and products are being introduced. When they do take place, they are taken very seriously. In the private sector, the atmosphere is comparable to the Western-style presentation, where disruptions are unlikely and time constraints apply.

When dealing with the government and traditional family businesses, however, older patterns still apply, and you are likely to be frequently interrupted by phone calls, doors opening and closing, and people bringing in papers for signature. Be patient. This does not indicate that your business is unimportant, but in this culture, people juggle many things at once.

Although it depends on the situation, it is rare for the top decision-maker to attend presentations, though this may also be affected by the amount of business you are bringing to the company. Generally, it is middle management or heads of department who will be present. Spend five or ten minutes making introductions and conversation. Once the presentation begins, avoid personal anecdotes and stories, and jokes. Egyptians do not always relate to Western humor but, if a foreigner makes a joke, they will be forced to laugh to avoid embarrassing them. Joking in a presentation setting creates awkwardness.

If the company chief is present, the formality factor increases, and the presentation will be short. Get straight to the point. If the top person receives a phone call, stop the presentation, and continue when they are ready.

The time you have for presentations depends very much on whom you are meeting, and the more senior the person the less time you have. Generally, presentations can run anywhere between fifteen minutes and an hour. It is wise to ask beforehand how much time has been allocated to prepare appropriately.

NEGOTIATIONS

It is important to be aware of two things when negotiating. First, the Arabic language and style is very flowery and expressive, and peppered with hyperbole. "Definitely" can mean "maybe." "Immediately" can mean "soon." It is sometimes wise not to take things too literally.

Second, many people will oversell at first, with the expectation that they will be knocked back. An Egyptian negotiator will be ready to reduce a price at the first sign of hesitation by the visitor. A visitor, on his part, should be prepared to inflate his proposals and be ready to bring them down. This shows a willingness to be flexible—a quality appreciated by Egyptians. When leaving the negotiating table, you should not consider that the negotiation is necessarily over. It is up to you to stay in touch regularly to keep the business relationship on track.

Negotiations will usually be conducted by middle management. They will communicate the results to senior management, who will close the deal and sign.

CONTRACTS

The Egyptian Civil Code is the prime source of civil law in Egypt. It is derived largely from the French Napoleonic

Code. While commercial provisions are included in the law, contracts should be comprehensive and set out all the details. The format will usually be dictated by the stronger party. Contracts will generally be in Arabic, except in rare cases with multinational companies where they will also be drafted in English. For court proceedings, English contracts should be translated into Arabic and notarized.

In Egypt, as in the West, contracts are binding, and disputes are settled in court. Court proceedings are lengthy and time-consuming, however, so it is recommended that provision for arbitration is included in any agreement. An Egyptian court will respect an arbitration clause. Arbitration may be conducted under any of the internationally recognized sets of rules.

WOMEN IN BUSINESS

Women in managerial positions still struggle to be accepted and taken seriously. While the law does not discriminate against women in work, society puts pressure on women to be a homemaker first and a professional second. The number of women in senior positions is increasing, but it is rare to find a woman with the final decision-making power in a large company.

Egyptian women expect to be treated as professional equals. However, guidelines for dealing with businesswomen differ dramatically from those with businessmen. Avoid any sign of intimacy. Inviting a female colleague out for dinner is a step beyond the norm.

WORKING SPACES

While internet and Wi-Fi access is available in most city cafés, some cafés may limit the time customers can use their premises as working spaces. There are many dedicated workspaces in all the major cities to accommodate travelers who need to work, and they are affordable and efficient.

SOCIALIZING

Egyptians are hospitable and look after their foreign visitors, but you are not likely to be invited into a contact's home as the domestic sphere is reserved for close friends and family. It is rare for spouses to attend business lunches and dinners.

No matter how Westernized the social setting, remember that this is a conservative society. Some businessmen may drink, but if you don't know that is the case, it is essential to wait for your contact to be the one to suggest alcohol.

Lunches and dinners start late in Egypt. Lunch can be served as late as 5:00 p.m. and dinner can be served at 10:00 p.m. To socialize over meals, one should be prepared to spend a lot of time outside the office. Generally, whoever has extended the invitation should pay the bill.

CHAPTER NINE

COMMUNICATING

LANGUAGE

Egypt's recent past is reflected in the languages spoken in the country today, and in cities such as Cairo, Alexandria, and Port Said it is common to find street names written in both Arabic and English, or Arabic and French.

Al-Arabiya al-fus'ha (Modern Standard Arabic) is the official language used in government, the media, and education. The vernacular Arabic spoken in Egypt is called *masry* (Egyptian colloquial dialect), and is a dialect of Modern Standard Arabic. *Masry* is what people speak in their homes and in everyday conversation with friends, and in markets and shops.

Other regional dialects exist and these are collectively called *al 'ammiyyah* (common) Arabic. Sa'idi Arabic is the main spoken language of southern Egypt. There are almost half a million speakers of the Nubian languages of Nobiin and Kenuzi among the Egyptians living around Kom Ombo and Aswan, in the far-southern Upper Nile Valley, and Siwi, a version of the Berber language of North

Africa, is spoken by Egyptian Berbers living in and around the Siwa Oasis.

Egyptian Sign Language has gained traction in the main cities of Cairo and Alexandria.

Most educated people in Egypt study English and speak it with their friends, with either an American or British accent. There are many English-language universities in the country, and English is the most widely used language in tourism. The Egyptian youth increasingly speak *masry* incorporating English words. Stamps and banknotes are printed in both English and Arabic.

Egypt has many visitors and residents from the Arab world, and trying to distinguish between *masry* and the vernaculars from, say, Libya, Jordan, or Saudi Arabia can be frustrating. These dialects differ greatly from country to country. However, because Egyptian films and TV series dominate in the Arab world, the Egyptian dialect is understood by most other Arabic-speaking nations.

Many travelers wanting to visit Arabic-speaking lands learn Modern Standard Arabic, which is understood in all these countries. There are language courses in Egypt offering both MSA and colloquial Egyptian. Some do tailor-made packages that include both. Online expat groups usually have listings of language classes and Arabic tutors. Embassies, too, have information on good Arabic tutors.

In areas frequented by tourists many people speak basic English, and some foreigners find themselves able to get by in Egypt without a single word of Arabic. But Egyptians warmly appreciate the efforts of those who try to speak their language. Making mistakes is fine—it is found quite charming—and people will extend more courtesy to foreigners who have made the effort to learn some Arabic, even a few words.

The Westernized upper classes generally speak English, and many speak French as well. In fact, eavesdrop at any upmarket café and watch as the customers dip in and out of different languages in a single sentence, communicating in some sort of Arabic–English mix.

GOOD MANNERS

In Egypt, attitude overrides vocabulary. The Egyptians are polite, and good manners govern their every interaction. True engagement with Egyptian society is possible for a foreigner who has understood and reciprocates these courtesies. Respect lies at the heart of good manners and addressing people by their correct title and showing deference to seniority in position and age is the norm.

Egyptians are helpful by nature. If asked for something, they must oblige. And sometimes they will do so even when not asked. For example, ask for directions in the street and, before you know it, a crowd has gathered and is engaged in debate about the best possible route for you.

Egyptian men may not open a door or pull out a chair for a woman. Their idea of gallantry is one of protection. A foreign woman should not be offended if her Egyptian male companion walks in front of her in the street rather than next to her, because he is trying to shield her from the crowds. An Egyptian man will never let a woman walk to her car alone after an evening out and is unlikely to allow her to take a cab home unaccompanied.

Always Offer!
Many Egyptians smoke and it is generally
allowed; however, smoking is no longer
permitted in hospitals or on public
transportation. An Egyptian smoker will
always offer cigarettes to others. In fact,
they will always offer whatever they have to
those present. However, the older generation,
particularly, disapproves of women smoking in
public. Women mainly smoke publicly in the
fashionable cafés and bars of the larger cities.

People behave conservatively in public. As we've
seen, displays of affection between members of the
opposite sex are taboo, mainly to protect a woman's
honor, but can be seen among the youth in certain
affluent areas as they become more Westernized.
Women who express their emotions loudly in public
spaces are considered rude. At the same time, it is
common to see two men hugging and kissing in the
street or walking down the street holding hands (with
no suggestion of a sexual relationship).

Egyptians generally speak loudly; this is considered
a sign of strength, while speaking softly indicates
hesitation. People make eye contact when talking—
it shows interest and trust. Someone who doesn't
make eye contact is considered untrustworthy. This
assertiveness is limited to the volume of speech, but
other forms of behavior, such as being direct and
forward, which are considered positive in the West,

are seen as aggressive and rude. Diplomacy is key to effective communication.

In conversation, good posture is important. Slouching shows a lack of respect. Putting your feet up or crossing your legs in a way that exposes the soles of your shoes is incredibly rude, especially in front of seniors. When in a group setting, presenting your back to someone is rude, and if you must do so for whatever reason, you should apologize to the person you are doing it to.

The sense of personal space in Egypt differs from that in the West. People tend to sit closer to each other and may be more tactile, but not with the opposite sex. Don't back away—this would imply that you find your counterpart offensive and would make you appear cold. Warmth is important. Hand gestures are common and are often used to emphasize a point.

THE MEDIA

Egypt has long enjoyed the reputation of cultural capital of the Arab world. It is home to the largest publishing houses in the region. Egypt's oldest newspaper, *Al Ahram*, together with *Al Akhbar* and *Al Gomhouria*, are the three main government-owned newspapers and those with the largest circulations. Several independent papers also exist, including the liberal *Al-Shorouk* and *Al-Masry Al-Youm*, which have a smaller circulation but are read by the country's decision-makers. Many weekly and monthly newspapers and magazines are published in Egypt and are widely available at newsstands and bookshops. All newspapers and magazines are subject to review by the government's Supreme Press Council.

Arabic satellite television broadcasters have boomed in recent years, with Al-Jazeera and Al-Arabiya covering regional events, and local channels such as ONTV and Dream TV more focused on Egypt.

The revolution that toppled Mubarak paved the way for a brief show of fearlessness in the media and the press, but human rights organizations are pressing for the laws on freedom of expression to be properly applied.

SERVICES

Telephone

The Egyptian telephone system is efficient, making calling just about anywhere in the world as easy as in the West. For directory inquiries, dial 140 from any landline or cell phone.

Cell phone networks work on landline, broadband, and 4G, and cover most of the country. Almost everyone owns a cell phone if not two. There are currently four cell phone networks in the country–Vodafone, Etisalat, Orange, and WE. Prepaid cards are available at many shops and kiosks. Getting a postpaid line requires some paperwork but can be done.

Pay phones are few and far between. If you have an emergency almost any Egyptian will allow you to use their mobile phone to make a call.

Mail

Egypt's postal system could claim to date back more than 4,000 years—the Ancient Egyptians used a system of couriers to deliver messages and goods throughout the kingdom, and even had a god of the postal service, Thoth (later identified with the Greek god Hermes).

The modern postal system was established in 1865 during Khedive Ismail's reign. The first post office was opened in Alexandria, followed by Cairo, Port Said, and other major cities. Today the service is operated by Egypt Post, a subsidiary of the Ministry of Communications and Information Technology. It provides traditional social and postal services such as mail, postage stamps, savings accounts, parcels, and pension disbursement, and now delivers digital services.

Egypt's postal system is typical of any developing country, and a small percentage of letters or packages may not arrive, so when sending something important, such as documents, it is best to use registered mail at the local post office. All packages are opened at customs. Books will often be checked for illegal material and CDs are treated with suspicion. Sometimes items in packages might go astray; this depends very much on their resale value.

It's best to send letters from a major city or hotel. Stamps can be purchased at post offices or hotels. Private courier firms such as Federal Express or DHL are limited to a few cities and are a lot more expensive.

Mail sent to you should bear your name, apartment or house number, and street name, followed by the area, then city, the five-digit postal code, and finally country.

Internet

The last two decades have seen an internet boom in Egypt, with internet access available in almost all areas.

In homes, anyone with a phone line and a modem can connect to the internet. Many cafés have high-speed connections and free wireless connection. Usually there will be a sign if the café has Wi-Fi; however, in some places it is becoming increasingly common to prohibit the use of Wi-Fi in cafés after 2:00 p.m. (peak time for cafés) as online users limit table turnaround.

The internet played an immense role in the 2011 Revolution. Activists, who were tightly monitored by Mubarak's security forces, were able to organize and mobilize through social networking sites such as Facebook and Twitter. The scale of the social networking took officials by surprise. They struggled to match the organization of the activists and briefly employed their own cyber-agents to engage in an online war with the pro-democracy activists.

Today social networking sites have brought a great sense of freedom to communication.

Social Media
Social media sites are commonly used by teenagers and adults who socialize online due to restrictions on dating and because it's convenient. Facebook, Twitter, and TikTok sites are popular, but Instagram is probably the most popular platform among youth with a penchant for selfies. As there are limited forms of entertainment, an outing to the seaside is considered a social event, and a selfie captures the moment.

Messaging and Voice Calls
WhatsApp and FB Messenger are used for messaging, but voice calls are often suspended on WhatsApp due to security concerns, and therefore Messenger is the best platform to use for voice or video calls.

CONCLUSION

Visiting and living in Egypt are very different experiences for foreigners, with the latter made possible only by the Egyptians' warm embrace of foreigners. The Egyptian people are welcoming, friendly, and relaxed. On the surface, the lifestyle of the moneyed classes is much the same as in the West, but we have seen some of the more subtle and complex aspects of their culture.

Daily, most Egyptians endure difficult conditions and remain resilient, taking life's knocks and springing back with humor and good nature. Despite the access of many to tertiary education and expertise, the great jobs still go to those with *wasta* (connections). Most Egyptians live at subsistence level, their value typically underappreciated, their expertise unacknowledged. Even in the corporate sector salaries may barely cover the basics. There is a huge untapped potential waiting to be recognized and rewarded, and Egypt could achieve greatness again if a solution could be found to the poverty affecting so many of its people.

The Egyptians' apparent passivity and fatalism, which can sometimes leave foreigners frustrated, is more than balanced by their good humor and positive outlook, and by their abiding belief that everything that happens in their lives, good or bad, is the will of Allah. They value good relationships, they are loyal to their friends, and are welcoming to their visitors. As the saying goes, "Anyone who drinks from the water of the Nile is sure to return."

FURTHER READING

Abdelmegiud, Ibrahim. *No One Sleeps in Alexandria*. Cairo: The American University in Cairo Press, 2007.

Alaswany, Alaa. *The Yacoubian Building*. London: HarperCollins, 2007.

Brier, Bob. *Egyptomania: Our Three Thousand Year Obsession with the Land of the Pharaohs*. New York: St. Martin's Press, 2013.

Durrell, Lawrence. *The Alexandria Quartet*. London: Faber & Faber, 2020.

El-Fiki, Shereen. *Sex and The Citadel: Intimate Life in a Changing Arab World*. London: Vintage, 2017.

Lane, Edward William. *An Account of the Manners and Customs of the Modern Egyptians*. Cairo: The American University in Cairo Press, 2003 (facsimile of 5th edition, 1865).

Mahfouz, Naguib. *Palace Walk*. New York: Anchor, 2011 (reprint).

Manley, Bill. *The Penquin Historical Atlas of Ancient Egypt*. London/New York: Penguin, 1997.

Miles, Hugh. *Playing Cards in Cairo*. London: Abacus, 2011.

Osman, Tarek. *Egypt on the Brink. From Nasser to the Muslim Brotherhood*. New Haven, CT/London: Yale University Press, 2013.

Pinch, Geraldine. *Egyptian Mythology: A Guide to the Gods, Goddesses, and Traditions of Ancient Egypt*. Oxford: OUP, 2004.

Rodenbeck, Max. *Cairo: The City Victorious*. London: Vintage, 2000.

Shaw, Ian. *Ancient Egypt: A Very Short Introduction*. Oxford: OUP, 2021.

Tignor, Robert L. *Egypt: A Short History*. Princeton, NJ: Princeton University Press, 2011.

Verner, Miroslav. *The Pyramids: The Mystery, Culture, and Science of Egypt's Great Monuments*. New York: Grove Press, 2007.

Wilkinson, Toby. *The Nile: A Journey Downriver Through Egypt's Past and Present*. New York/London: Vintage, 2015.

USEFUL APPS

Egypt is one of the most internet-savvy countries in Africa. You can order almost anything online or access many services via phone apps. Here is a list of some of the most popular apps to get you started.

Travel and Transportation

Hail a ride with **Uber**, **Careem**, **inDriver**, and **Didi**. Share rides on **Swivl** minibuses. Journey plan and buy tickets with **Mobility Cairo**. Navigate with **Google Maps**.

Food and Shopping

Shop general items on **Souq**, **Jumia**, **Amazon.eg**, and **Noon**. Order groceries and household items with **Instashop** and **Breadfast** who delivers these plus freshly baked bread. Higher-end produce can be found on **Gourmet**. Restaurant meals can be ordered for delivery via **Talabat** and **Elmenus**.

Communication and Banking

Buy and manage SIMs and phone plans via **Ana Vodafone** and **My Orange**. Make payments with **InstaPay** and **My Etisalat**.

Health

Book a consultation or home visit with a doctor using **Vezeete**. Prescription and over-the-counter medicines can be ordered for delivery using **Yodawy** and **Chefaa**.

PICTURE CREDITS

Cover image: *General view of pyramids in Giza.* © Shutterstock/Kanuman

Shutterstock: 12 by marwa m. dakhakhny; 14, 18, 19 by AlexAnton; 16 by fogcatcher; 20 (left and right) by M. Farouk; 82 by Bembo De Niro; 85 by MaguedM; 86 by Novie Charlene Magne; 90 (left) by Viacheslav Lopatin; 90 (right), 141 (left) by Dina Saeed; 96 by Orhan Cam; 100 by leshiy985; 103 by Ebtikar; 107 by Moatassem; 108 by ebonyeg; 111 by Nataliya Derkach; 124 by rafik beshay; 129 by John Wreford; 132 by ebonyeg; 134 by Kozlik; 136 by Tunatura; 137 by Melnikov Dmitriy; 139, 157 by Sun_Shine; 141 (right) by hussein farar; 144 by Matyas Rehak; 145 by Emily Marie Wilson; 158 by Thomas Wyness; 184 by Ibnburhan; 189 by Emad Omar Farouk; 194 by Fedor Selivanov.

Unsplash: pages 12, 128 by Alex Azabache; 60 by ARTISTIC FRAMES; 98 by Flo P; 123 by Khaled Ghareeb; 150 by Noel Schläfli; 168 by Omar Elsharawy.

Creative Commons Attribution-Share Alike 4.0 International license: page 26 © Moh hakem; 28 © José Luiz.

INDEX

Acknowledgments

With special thanks to Christopher, Matthew, and Nicholas Morris, and
Caitlyn Barone for their unfailing support; to Mohamed Kamal for fact-
checking; to Jailan Zayan for a framework on which to build; Geoffrey Chesler
for his thorough editing; Amanda Hardy for introducing me to Egypt; and to
the Egyptians who made me want to return, and who keep me here.